WHEN THE CENTER DOES NOT HOLD

Leading in an Age of Polarization

David R. Brubaker, with Everett N. Brubaker, Carolyn E. Yoder, and Teresa J. Haase

Fortress Press
Minneapolis

When the Center Does Not Hold

WHEN THE CENTER DOES NOT HOLD
Leading in an Age of Polarization

Print ISBN: 978-1-5064-5305-7
eBook ISBN: 978-1-5064-5306-4

Cover image: © iStock 2019; Radial Scatter Abstract Vector Round Particles – Illustration by yamonstro
Cover design: Alisha Lofgren

CONTENTS

PREFACE

"Relationships matter." That was the mantra of the conflict transformation movement I joined in 1986. My spouse, Martha Neff Brubaker, and I had just returned from a term of service with Mennonite Central Committee (MCC) in northeastern Brazil, and I had accepted the position of associate director with Mennonite Conciliation Service (MCS), based in MCC's headquarters in Akron, Pennsylvania.

My two years with MCS were filled with new experiences—practicing the process and skills of mediation, consulting with conflicted congregations, and editing a quarterly journal (*Conciliation Quarterly*) that mapped the contours of this emerging movement. As a new mediator and consultant, I was convinced that my toolkit was adequate for any conflict. "Have process, will travel," as a friend summarized.

My own great awakening came in 1990, when I became aware through a family member of a sexual abuse crisis within my own denomination (not Mennonite). Working with other family members, we organized a "Victims Advocacy Group" to provide support for the survivors of the abuse crisis. We met monthly to listen to the survivors' stories and plan together how to respond. The survivors' main concerns were greater protection against future victimization and increased awareness among church leaders regarding how to respond to allegations of sexual abuse.

After a meeting with the governing board of the impacted denomination, I realized I was filled with anger regarding the leaders' treatment of the survivors. Rather than focus on the harm that survivors had experienced and the need to ensure there would be no future victims, the church leaders seemed obsessed with protecting the reputation of the institution and defending their own handling of the situation.

In the coming months, the anger transformed into genuine rage. When our Victims Advocacy Group gathered, the conversation inevitably devolved into laments about the church leaders' ignorance and into accusations regarding their behavior and character. From various accounts, I learned that the church leaders were themselves sharing similar laments and accusations about our group. The critical challenge of responding to sexual abuse was soon buried under personal animus and ad hominem attacks. In short, we had polarized.

I share this story not to criticize our Victims Advocacy Group, which I think provided critical support to the survivors of a church counselor's extensive and long-standing sexual misconduct. Instead, I share it to acknowledge that the net of polarization can snare all of us—even those ostensibly most committed to preserving relationships. While mediating disputes between friends and colleagues, urging them to be "hard on issues but soft on people," I was also raging against church leaders.

The instinct to polarize is a natural human response to high-intensity conflict. Such conflict produces anxiety and alienation, and when those feelings surface, we naturally seek allies. The instinct to pull back from those with whom we are in conflict and to huddle instead with those who believe as we do is understandable. We are, after all, tribal creatures. The homophily principle ("birds of a feather flock together") soars high when we feel threatened or isolated.[1]

If polarization is our natural response, how do we divert from that course in high-level conflict? My own experience, as both a participant and an intervener in polarized conflicts, is that we can either strive to prevent conflict from escalating or attempt to deescalate it once relationships have polarized. Either way, we eventually have to address the root causes of polarization (which we will explore in chapter 1 of this book).

While my experience as a mediator and consultant since 1986 provides me with some qualifications to address polarization, I bring limitations as well. For example, I am a white, straight, sixty-something, Christian male, and my experience with religious organizations has been primarily in white Christian institutions (although I have had the privilege of consulting with an ashram and a synagogue, as well as with a number of secular organizations). Thus, my own positionality and life experience limit my understanding of the impact of polarization on racial, religious, and sexual minorities in this country.

To partially offset my limitations in terms of age, gender, and expertise, I have invited three individuals to contribute chapters to this book. Everett Brubaker, who possesses an MA in communication and advocacy and is also my son, writes about communicating across the divide. Carolyn Yoder, founding director of the globally known Strategies for Trauma Awareness (STAR) program, addresses trauma and polarization. And Teresa Haase, a professor and counselor, unpacks the need for leaders to practice resilience in the face of polarization.

None of the four of us claims to know the magic key to depolarizing our current highly polarized society. We will, however, share our insights from the research and writing on this topic and our own experiences of living and working in polarized environments. Some of what we share may resonate with you. If it does, we'd love to hear from you. And if it doesn't, we would welcome your insights as to what we're missing.

Our primary hope is that this book will contribute to the growing body of knowledge and practices regarding how our increasingly diverse human communities might not merely coexist but thrive together. Many forces conspire to drive us apart. Building the capacity to stay together despite our differences will require personal, organizational, communal, and societal transformation. Perhaps the greatest transformation that will be needed is in our capacity to love.

David R. Brubaker
June 2019

Notes

1. Miller McPherson, Lynn Smith Lovin, and James M. Cook, "Birds of a Feather: Homophily in Social Networks," *Annual Review of Sociology* 27 (August 2001): 415–44, https://tinyurl.com/y4ur4ypm.

ACKNOWLEDGMENTS

This is the third book I have written since completing graduate work in 2007, and the process of producing it was the most collaborative of the three. I'm particularly grateful to the three chapter authors—Teresa J. Haase, Everett N. Brubaker, and Carolyn E. Yoder—for producing such relevant content in a relatively short timeframe. They filled in significant gaps in my own knowledge base—around communication, trauma, and resilience—which greatly enhanced the content of this book.

I'm also very grateful to my academic colleagues at Eastern Mennonite University (EMU), both in the Department of Business and Leadership and the Center for Justice and Peacebuilding (CJP). They supported me in taking Fridays at home to write during the 2018/2019 academic year, and several provided significant insights into the dynamics of polarization and what is required of leaders in this age of polarization.

While she was a student, CJP alumna Lenore Bajare Dukes worked with me to conceptualize the outline of this book and also interviewed former EMU president Loren Swartzendruber (featured in chapter 2). Dukes's contributions to this work far exceed the one quote that I've been able to include from her.

My consulting colleagues with the Congregational Consulting Group endorsed my proposal to offer a five-part series on polarization within our weekly e-zine, *Perspectives*. This gave me an opportunity to test both the proposed causes of polarization and potential remedies, which evolved to become the core content of chapter 1 and chapter 6 of this book.

The more than one hundred organizational and congregational clients I've been privileged to work with since 1987 have served as priceless teachers for me. I'm especially appreciative of the dozens of "reference teams" I've worked with in longer-term conflict interventions. Their insights on proactively building resilient systems, deescalating high-intensity conflict, and recovering post-conflict have consistently proven more valuable in their particular context than anything I've read (or written).

Over the last few years, I've come to respect and value the other five members of our "Gang of Six" from Park View Mennonite Church in Harrisonburg, Virginia: Margaret Foth, Vernon Jantzi, Edgar Miller, Mark Nissley, and Marcia Pusey. As I mention in chapter 7, this group of members with diverse perspectives meets once a month to identify our many shared values and also to talk openly about areas where we differ. We began our process with an opportunity for each member to share their life story, which helped to solidify our relationships prior to discussing differences.

Most importantly, I'm deeply grateful to my spouse, Martha (Mert) Neff Brubaker; our sons, Everett and Emerson; and our daughter-in-law, Kelsey. The five of us were delighted to welcome Loam Oliver to this world in January of 2019, and I'm awed by Kelsey and Everett's patience and creativity as new parents. I've learned more from my family about the power of love and about staying connected despite differences than I have from my graduate studies or even from my clients. That's because our families challenge our deepest beliefs and values about love and commitment in ways that professional relationships never quite achieve.

Finally, I want to express my sincere appreciation to the very capable staff at Fortress Press who enabled the production of this book. I particularly want to thank Beth Gaede, senior acquisitions editor, who is an exceptional editor and "clarity coach." Allyce Amidon served as the project manager for this book. My entire experience with Fortress Press has been characterized by competence and compassion. Any errors or omissions in the text are my responsibility, however, as Fortress provided ample opportunity to review the manuscript before printing.

Polarization dynamics result when conflict escalates and the parties involved are unwilling or unable to find an agreement or accommodation that satisfies them both. Polarization is thus a normal human process, albeit generally a very painful one. My prayer in releasing this book is that those of us who wrote it and those of you who read it would all commit to depolarizing attitudes and behaviors. In the current climate in the United States, this would be a radically countercultural act.

INTRODUCTION

> Things fall apart; the center cannot hold;
> Mere anarchy is loosed upon the world,
> The blood-dimmed tide is loosed, and everywhere
> The ceremony of innocence is drowned;
> The best lack all conviction, while the worst
> Are full of passionate intensity.
> Surely some revelation is at hand;
> Surely the Second Coming is at hand.
>
> —W. B. Yeats, 1919

Bishop Dinis Sengulane, known as the "Archbishop Tutu of Mozambique," offered courageous leadership for peace in the midst of violent conflict. Like Archbishop Desmond Tutu of South Africa, Bishop Sengulane provided leadership in a highly polarized society. His efforts at peacebuilding came after years of watching innocent church members and leaders be slain because of the ongoing civil war in his country.

> I got involved in the peace and reconciliation process because of the pastoral findings that I was making in my visits to several areas of the country. I would listen to people at the church door. . . . I would also listen to my colleagues from the other churches and felt it was not enough to be lamenting. We needed to do something.[1]

After Mozambique gained independence from Portugal in 1975 via a violent revolution, factional fighting plunged the country into a sixteen-year civil war. Anglican bishop Sengulane and his Catholic colleague, Archbishop Don Jaime Goncalves, helped convince the warring parties to participate in negotiations.

The two religious leaders prevailed on then-president Joaquim Chissano to permit them to initiate contacts with rebel party leaders. In 1989, four Catholic and Protestant church leaders, including Sengulane and Goncalves, met first with President Chissano in Maputo and then with a delegation of rebel leaders in Kenya. Additional meetings with both factions ultimately led to an agreement to meet in Rome for talks. Members of the Sant'Egidio community, a lay Catholic community in Rome, hosted representatives of the two warring factions for ten rounds of negotiations over a two-year period, resulting in the General Peace Accord of October 1992.

As Bishop Sengulane recalls, the success of this initiative was due in part to the collaboration between Protestant and Catholic leaders.

> Some of us had the feeling that the answer to the problem of war came through dialogue. We were a minority with a timid voice. . . . But we concluded that the people who killed and who were being killed were Mozambicans. Therefore, the matter needed to be solved by the Mozambicans themselves. The only thing that came from outside were the arms and the ideology. We from the CCM [Christian Council of Mozambique, the association of Protestant churches] knew that the Catholic Church had the same concern. Therefore, we decided to put our hands together in a common project.[2]

In addition to this ecumenical partnership for peace, a second factor contributed to the success of the religious leaders' efforts. This was the insistence by CCM that their ordained members not become involved in partisan politics. While CCM leaders issued pastoral letters calling for an end to violence, they also modeled political impartiality and urged pastors to do the same. As Bishop Sengulane noted, "We human beings are political, but we cannot become instruments of the politicians. . . . We are political beings but cannot be prisoners of politics."[3]

Bishop Sengulane's words apply to religious leaders throughout the world and particularly in the United States today. As "political beings," it is incumbent upon religious leaders to discern their own roles among the political dynamics affecting their congregations. One of the major dynamics is polarization. We live in a society in which political divisions run so deep that they affect almost every sphere of life—including families, congregations, and communities. In the remainder of this chapter, I explore the nature of polarization and how polarization permeates our lives and communities.

The Persistence of Polarization

Polarization refers to the process by which more and more people in a society come to hold opinions at the more extreme ends of the spectrum, while the number of people in the moderate center dwindles. Polarization is both a global and a historic phenomenon, as it has surfaced in many countries and at numerous points in history.

We choose to focus primarily on the United States in this book, as that is our own context and a country where polarization currently confronts leaders at all levels. The US has experienced profound polarization in every century of its history—including during the Revolutionary War, in the run-up to the Civil War, and in the late 1960s.

In the American Revolution, not all of the colonists were "patriots." Many remained loyal to the crown and were condemned as "Tories" by their revolutionary neighbors. Those who supported the rebellion considered them "persons inimical to the liberties of America,"[4] and about 80,000 loyalists fled to Canada or Britain during or after the war. The divisions between the "loyalists" and the "patriots" were both bitter and deep. Our country was birthed in a polarized cradle.

The decade preceding the American Civil War was also a time of deep partisanship and division. The country was on the brink of civil war by 1850. Though the Compromise of 1850 managed to forestall actual shooting for a decade,[5] it failed to resolve the stark differences between the slave-owning Southern states and the so-called free states of the North, particularly as westward expansion continued and the status of western territories polarized the country.

Finally, the 1960s was a profoundly polarized decade, as the struggle over civil rights intensified and protesters denounced the war in Vietnam. I believe the turmoil of the 1960s and early 1970s set the stage for our current era of polarization. Those of us in the baby-boom generation were shaped in the turmoil of the 1960s. Some of us fought in Vietnam while others protested the war. Some of us marched with Martin Luther King Jr. while others decried civil unrest. Some of our sisters and brothers died at Kent State while some of our brothers were among the National Guard troops who fired the fatal bullets. The baby-boom generation, like our nation, was polarized from its inception. And it is members of the baby-boom generation who now occupy the majority of leadership roles in business, education, health care, and government.

Political polarization appears most dramatically in the United States Congress, where Democratic and Republican representatives (particularly in the House of Representatives) increasingly vote in purely party-line fashion. The shift from the 1950s to today has been dramatic, as various visuals portray.[6] Our elected representatives' increasing division both reflects and contributes to increasing polarization among the electorate.

Numerous studies have charted increasing polarization among the US public over the past four decades. The partisan divide has widened in every presidential election since the mid-1970s. According to political science professor Alan Abramowitz of

Emory University, "The divisions between red [Republican] states and blue [Democratic] states are far deeper today than they were 30 or 40 years ago."[7]

Multiple demographic variables underlie the political divisions. According to Abramowitz, "The most important divide within the contemporary electorate . . . is the racial divide,"[8] followed closely by a regional divide, an urban–rural divide, a gender gap, a marriage gap, and a religious-commitment gap. As a broadly accurate generalization, a married, Southern, rural, white man who attends religious services regularly is likely to vote Republican. A single, Northern, urban woman of color who only occasionally attends a religious service is equally likely to vote Democratic.

Yet, we must be cautious when correlating identity (based on demographic variables) and voting patterns, as every individual possesses multiple intersecting identities. *Intersectionality* refers to the fact that all people possess multiple identities (race, gender, class, and so forth) at the same time. This reality has a complex effect on any individual's experience of power, privilege, and oppression. Individuals may experience privilege due to one aspect of their identity (for instance, race) and disempowerment along another (for instance, class). The intersection of identities requires us to develop a more nuanced understanding of the role of identity and polarization.

Abramowitz offers another sobering finding about the extent of polarization in the United States today: "The more engaged Americans are in the political process—the more they care about politics, the more they know about politics, and the more they participate in politics—the more partisan and the more polarized they tend to be."[9] By contrast, the least polarized citizens in the United States are also the most politically apathetic.

Are there no alternatives to active political engagement and increasing polarization versus complete political withdrawal and attendant apathy? Are leaders condemned to either engage in the fray and fight for their political preferences or withdraw from the battlefield and cede territory to the shrillest voices? Before we can respond, we need to understand how polarization functions.

How Does Polarization Work?

Polarization can occur in any social system—a family, a community, an organization, or a society. Moreover, because every social system is embedded in a larger social system, polarization at one level may contribute to polarization at other levels. The classic "nested model of conflict" (figure 1) developed in 1996 by conflict theorist Maire Dugan demonstrates this reality.[10]

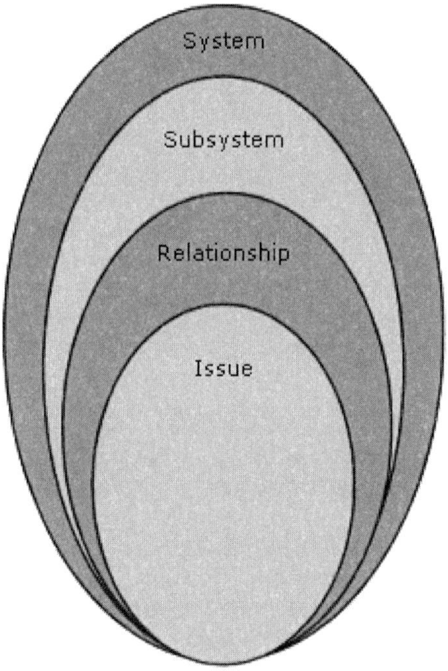

A Nested Model of Conflict

At the micro level, we can imagine divisive conflicts over specific issues, such as gun violence, abortion, and immigration. All of those issues, however, are embedded in the context of specific relationships—whether interpersonal or inter-group. In addition, those relational conflicts are themselves nested in specific subsystems, such as communities, organizations, and congregations. Finally, every subsystem is part of a larger system, whether regional, national, or global.

The significance of a nested model is that it demonstrates how polarization can occur in both a downward and an upward direction. If a society polarizes over issues such as gun violence, abortion, or immigration, the polarization will affect every subsystem and relationship in that society. Individuals and groups will feel tremendous pressure to choose to be either "pro-gun, pro-life, and pro-wall" or "pro-gun control, pro-choice, and pro-immigration." Likewise, increasing polarization at the relational level will affect societal polarization.

We also can diagnose when polarization has occurred based on the "Levels of Conflict" model (figure 2). Developed by Speed Leas, longtime senior consultant with the Alban Institute, based on his decades of work with conflict in congregations, this model identifies five levels of conflict, as follows:

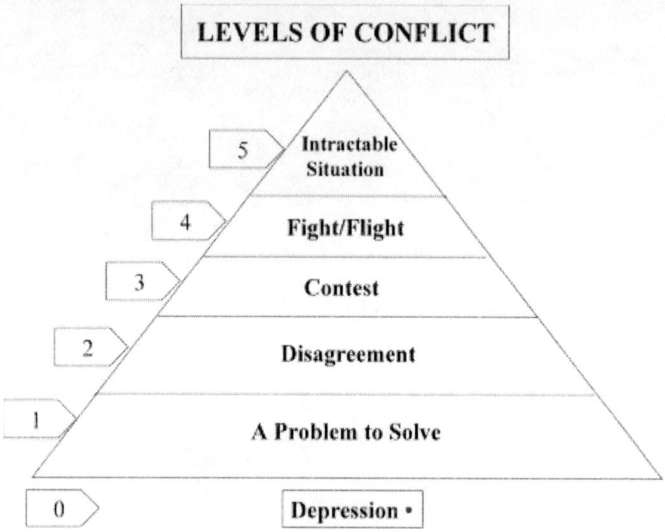

Leas's Levels of Conflict

Level One: A Problem to Solve

Conflicting goals, values, needs. Problem oriented rather than person oriented.

Level Two: Disagreement

Mixing of personalities and issues, problem cannot be clearly defined. Beginning of distrust and personalizing problem.

Level Three: Contest

Begin the dynamics of "win/lose." Personal attacks. Formation of factions, sides, camps. Distortion a major problem.

Level Four: Fight/Flight

Shifts from winning to getting rid of person(s). Factions are solidified. Talk now takes on the language of "principles," not "issues."

> **Level Five: Intractable Situation**
>
> No longer clear understanding of issue(s); personalities have become the focus. Conflict is now unmanageable. Energy is centered on the elimination and/or destruction of the person(s).
>
> **Level Zero: Depression**
>
> Depression is defined as "anger turned inward." Sometimes congregations do not know they are in conflict because they are in a state of depression. The task is to raise their awareness that there are problems to be solved.[11]

Polarization dynamics start to emerge in Level Three conflict ("Contest") but become blatant in Level Four ("Fight/Flight") as factions form and efforts manifest to purge opponents and the uncommitted. By the time a conflict reaches Level Five ("Intractable"), the desire is not just to purge but also to rid the earth of the "unbelievers." Efforts to combat polarization, then, are most effective when conflict is at Level Two or Three and more amenable to resolution. When conflict has reached Level Four or Five, other approaches (which will be discussed later) are indicated. As of this writing in mid-May 2019, I believe that the United States as a whole is at a very high Level Four conflict, with some individuals and groups engaged in Level Five conflict.

Results of Polarization

Polarization emerges at Level Four ("Fight/Flight") and tends to produce a schism at Level Five ("Intractable"). When a congregation or other organization is polarized, we see a range of predictable behaviors, all of which are discussed in Speed Leas's classic treatise on the five levels of conflict.

First, when a system polarizes, individuals retreat into discrete "affinity groups" that share common beliefs and values, and they tend to cut off relationships with those who don't share their stance. Negotiation with other groups (and particularly, compromise) is viewed as "selling out" the group's basic principles. (Consider, for example, the "Freedom Caucus" that has emerged in the US House of Representatives.) Any encounter with different opinions or perspectives is viewed in win/lose terms—and in very high-level conflict may even be phrased in apocalyptic language: "If they win the election our country will be destroyed!" In Level Four conflict, the goal is to overcome the opposition and (ideally) drive their members out of the system. In those rare conflicts that reach Level Five, the goal is to eliminate the "evildoers" altogether.

Second, the focus in high-level conflict shifts from "issues" to "personalities." I've intervened in several dozen Level Four conflicts in congregations, and in nearly every case the clergyperson had become the "identified patient"—at least for a significant group within the congregation. Whatever issues might have dominated the discussion at earlier levels have by Level Four generally devolved into ad hominem attacks. The maxim of principled negotiation (to be "hard on issues, but soft on people") is either ignored or trampled by combatants at Levels Four and Five, because they have personalized the conflict. We may still fuss about "the issues" at these higher levels of conflict, but at a more profound level we have imprinted the face of the enemy.

Third, any information that does not support one's "position" is either ignored or discredited. Although it's easy to see this operating in the public sphere ("The story was on MSNBC/Fox News, so I know it's fiction!"), it happens just as clearly in individual congregations and religious systems. This is why simply assembling people for "dialogue" in highly conflicted systems is at best unproductive and at worst harmful. By Levels Four and Five, it doesn't matter to the combatants *what* is being communicated so much as *who* is communicating. The plaintive call for "more information" or "better education on the issues" is understandable but also unproductive at these high levels of conflict. The brain seems unable to receive information from an individual or group it considers "the enemy," and it dismisses information that contradicts strongly held beliefs regardless of the source.

Whether in a family, an organization, or a society, polarization tends to damage or destroy existing relationships. John Paul Lederach, veteran peacebuilder and a key founder of the Center for Justice and Peacebuilding at Eastern Mennonite University, suggests that polarization produces a new equilibrium. In essence, the social structure changes after a polarizing experience—whether a divorce in a family unit or a civil war in a nation.

While polarization always transforms relationships, it is impossible to predict at the outset the form those relationships will take post-polarization. Civil conflict, for example, can produce two countries (e.g., South Sudan and Sudan) or a "reunited" but deeply wounded single country (e.g., the United States following the Civil War). All we can say with certainty is that polarization changes relationships. This means that the byproduct of a polarized family, congregation, community, or society will be a fundamentally transformed social system.

Responding to Polarization

Given this reality, how shall we live? I believe that leaders, at all levels, are the ones with the primary responsibility—and ability—to pull us back from the brink. However, in order to do so, they will have to refuse the two primary temptations—fight and flight—that are the most common responses to polarization. We do not need more leaders who either deepen our divisions or refuse to address them.

Rather, we need leaders with the ability to be both utterly clear about who they are and what they believe and, paradoxically, equally interested in the experiences and beliefs of others in the systems they lead. This is because the antidote to polarization is not conflict avoidance but conflict engagement.

Are you called to lead in such a time as this? If so, you will be unable to avoid dealing with deep polarization. Instead, you will be required to voice your truth and clarify your deepest principles, while listening intently and sincerely to those whose truth and principles differ. We need leaders who will offer us not fear but hope. Hope requires that we:

Humanize our opponents
Openly state our core beliefs
Pursue justice (particularly racial, gender, and economic justice)
Engage difference

The antidote to polarization is neither fight nor flight. Rather, the current perilous times require leaders who are both transparent and invitational. Tell us what you believe and why, and invite us to do the same. Doing so builds trust—the most important leadership currency.

Chapter Outline

What causes polarization, and what can be done about it? Any complex social phenomenon, including polarization, requires an examination of multiple causal variables. Chapter 1, "Understanding Polarization," addresses ten possible causes of polarization—ranging from economic inequality to leadership-driven polarization—and identifies one combination of factors that produces societal polarization.

In chapter 2, "Leadership and Polarization," we examine the impact of leading in an age of polarization on those entrusted with leadership roles. We then consider the commitments leaders must make in order to lead successfully in such an environment—commitments to clarity, compassion, courage, and connection.

Communication is the key process in both propelling and overcoming polarization. In chapter 3, "Communicating across the Divide," we explore how mindfulness around message, messenger, and audience can cultivate a communication climate that promotes deliberative dialogue rather than ritualistic debate.

In the flood of books on polarization, relatively little has surfaced regarding the role of trauma. In chapter 4, "Trauma, Polarization, and Connection," we consider the relationship between trauma and polarization, and the commitments necessary to be a truly reparative leader.

One of the greatest challenges leaders face in polarized systems is maintaining their own health and perspective. In chapter 5, "Weathering Polarization with Resilience," we contemplate the steps that leaders can take to survive and even thrive in an age of polarization.

Can polarization ever be overcome? In chapter 6, "Transforming Polarization," we consider methods to transform polarizing dynamics at the intrapersonal and interpersonal levels, as well as within our congregations, communities, and society.

We strive in this book to bring together insights from sociology, communication, trauma and resiliency studies, and our own experience. Join us on a journey toward understanding and transforming our polarized societies—one relationship and one system at a time.

Notes

1. Personal interview by the author, January 2012.
2. Personal interview by the author, January 2012.
3. Personal interview by the author, January 2012.
4. Wikipedia, s.v. "Loyalist (American Revolution)," last modified December 11, 2018, https://en.wikipedia.org/wiki/Loyalist_(American_Revolution).
5. Wikipedia, s.v. "Compromise of 1850," last modified December 28, 2018, https:// tinyurl.com/h662c9y.
6. See, for example, *Business Insider*, "The Rise of Partisanship in the House of Representatives" (60-sec. video), May 11, 2016, https://www.youtube.com/watch?v= tEczkhfLwqM.
7. Alan I. Abramowitz, *The Disappearing Center* (New Haven: Yale University Press, 2010), 100.
8. Abramowitz, *Disappearing Center*, 71.

9. Alan I. Abramowitz, *The Polarized Public? Why American Government Is So Dysfunctional* (Upper Saddle River, NJ: Pearson, 2013), 13.
10. Maire A. Dugan, "A Nested Theory of Conflict," *A Leadership Journal* 1 (July 1996).
11. "Levels of Conflict by Speed Leas," The Center for Congregational Health, September 1, 2011, http://tinyurl.com/y6applv3. Graph developed by Dr. Les Robinson during his tenure with the Center for Congregational Health, and based on Speed Leas' Levels of Conflict.

1

UNDERSTANDING POLARIZATION

David R. Brubaker

> A presidential election in the United States may be looked upon as a time of national crisis. Long before the date arrives, the election becomes everyone's major, not to say sole, preoccupation. The ardor of the various factions intensifies, and whatever artificial passions the imagination can create in a happy and tranquil country make their presence felt. . . . As the election draws near, intrigues intensify, and agitation increases and spreads. The citizens divide into several camps, each behind its candidate. A fever grips the entire nation.
>
> —Alexis de Tocqueville

Ed Harry is the son of a coal miner, a veteran of the war in Vietnam, and a resident of Luzerne County in Pennsylvania. He is one of twelve Luzerne County residents profiled by journalist Ben Bradlee Jr. in *The Forgotten: How the People of One Pennsylvania County Elected Donald Trump and Changed America.*

"I was a Democrat for fifty-two years of my life," Ed told Bradlee. "Then NAFTA and GATT happened and I became disillusioned." Luzerne County had been hemorrhaging jobs since coal mines began closing in the 1970s, while manufacturing jobs disappeared beginning in the 1980s. "I know a lot of people who lost jobs after all the manufacturers left," Ed lamented. "There was a mass migration out of here."[1]

In addition to globalization and trade agreements, Ed faults immigration for the setbacks his community and county have experienced. In 2016, Ed liked Donald Trump's plainspoken ways and his commitment to reducing both illegal and legal immigration. "No more trade agreements. And something had to be done with immigration."[2]

Ed is one among millions of mostly white men and women who flocked to candidate Trump in 2016. Their reasons for doing so included disillusionment with traditional politicians, concern about immigration (and the changing racial composition of the country), opposition to globalization (and the attendant loss of manufacturing jobs), and a pervasive fear that they are falling behind and have been forgotten.

Their fears are understandable. The country is changing demographically, millions of manufacturing jobs have been lost since 1980, and many working and middle-class Americans are indeed falling behind. Real income for most Americans has remained stagnant for some forty years, while the gap between the rich and the rest has grown dramatically.[3]

What Causes Polarization?

If leaders wish to address polarization, they must first understand its causes. Multiple theories have emerged to explain polarization, each of which may explain part of the phenomenon. Following are ten explanations offered in the literature on polarization, ranging from economic to psychological. We will examine several of these in later chapters, with a particular focus on how leaders might respond to these causal factors.

1. Economic Inequality

The single greatest culprit driving political polarization may be growing economic stratification. Income inequality in the United States in 2018 was higher than any time since the Great Depression and will likely only continue to increase.[4] While the post–World War II era was a time of rising prosperity for most Americans, beginning in the mid-1970s wealth began to accrue primarily at the very top. Regressive tax policies under successive presidential administrations have propelled this trend. Economists generally agree that "the tax positions of the Reagan and Bush administrations magnified income redistribution."[5]

Why does economic inequality matter? Because as the gap between the richest and the poorest citizens increases, political polarization rises. Political scientist Nolan McCarty and his colleagues chart this correlation in *Polarized America: The Dance of Ideology and Unequal Riches.* They demonstrate that the higher the income share of the top 1 percent, the greater the polarization in the US House of Representatives. When the income share of the top 1 percent increased from 8 percent to 18 percent between the 1970s and the 2000s, the polarization index (a measure of polarization among members in the House of Representatives) also more than doubled.[6]

Such correlation is equally evident at the macro level—across countries. Nations with the greatest gap between the rich and the poor (such as Brazil) tend to experience the highest levels of political polarization, whereas those with the smallest wealth gaps (such as in northern Europe) experience lower levels of polarization.[7]

The general robustness of income inequality as a predictor of political polarization is significant. It suggests that one of the best antidotes to polarization may be working for more progressive tax policies and flatter pay differentials. (The CEOs of the largest US corporations currently earn nearly 300 times as much as the average American worker.[8]) Large income differentials contribute to political polarization, as voters become vulnerable to grievance narratives from both the left and the right.

2. Identity Threats

Human beings are tribal creatures. Writer Sebastian Junger wondered why many white settlers in colonial-era America chose to stay with Indian tribes after they had been kidnapped. The answer, he concluded, was that when they were with the Indian tribe, they felt they belonged.[9] Belonging is a fundamental human need, as it allows us to claim an identity and a sense of safety by virtue of membership in a particular group.

Lilliana Mason, a professor of government at the University of Maryland, College Park, proposes that politics has become our new identity. Mason suggests that ideological, religious, and racial identities are increasingly clustered or "sorted," and thus, "partisanship can now be thought of as a mega-identity (encompassing all of the above)."[10]

The result of this clustering into partisan mega-identities is that "we have gone from two parties that are a little bit different in a lot of ways to two parties that are very different in a few powerful ways."[11] This merging of ethnic and religious identities with partisan affiliation may help explain why African American Catholics vote overwhelmingly for Democratic candidates and white evangelicals for Republican ones. When all of those in my "tribe" appear to be supporting a particular party or candidate, I find it hard to be an outlier.

Rather than forming intersecting alliances, where we agree with individuals on some issues but disagree with them on others, we develop sharply bifurcated allegiances. The danger is that "when multiple identities are strongly aligned, a threat to one identity affects the status of multiple other identities."[12] Polarization may result when individuals who share a common identity (e.g., conservative white Christians) fear that their status or their very identity is threatened.

Social identity theory with its concept of status threat helps us understand why voters might respond to a leader who promises to renew an identity group's status if it is declining or perceived to be declining.[13] In social identity theory, the groups with which we identify are an important source not only of belonging but also of self-esteem. Thus, individual members of an identity group are particularly likely to exhibit hostility toward other groups if they feel their status is threatened.

Yale law professor Amy Chua cites survey findings that more than half of white Americans believe whites have replaced blacks as victims of discrimination. The perceived status threat is heightened by the awareness that whites will soon become a demographic minority in the United States. These twin fears have produced a version of white identity politics "that has mobilized around the idea of whites as an endangered, discriminated-against group."[14]

Research has found that "typical responses to identity threats include ignoring information and perspectives that threaten the core identity, reinforcing affiliations with like-minded individuals and groups, and negatively characterizing outsiders."[15] These tendencies help us understand why identity threat and status threat fuel the processes of polarization. Among other policy responses, status threat makes many white voters more likely to favor limiting government (and its perceived ability to favor non-white groups) and to support more anti-immigration stances.

3. Racism and Racial Inequality

Racism may also be a significant implicit driver of polarization. The enslavement of Africans and the genocide against Native Americans represent the twin original sins that scarred the birth of this country. Although legalized slavery ended with the Thirteenth Amendment in 1865, and the Civil Rights Act of 1964 abolished

Jim Crow laws, racism continues to be a daily reality in the United States. As Princeton professor Eddie S. Glaude Jr. writes, "Americans have grown comfortable with racism resting just beneath the surface of our politics—to be activated whenever a politician or a community needed it, or some racist incident exhumed it only for us to bury it once again."[16]

Historian Jon Meacham traces the roots of modern polarization back to 1865 and the American Civil War. For Meacham, "Our history and our politics even now are unintelligible without first appreciating the roots of white Southern discontent about the verdict of the Civil War."[17] With other contemporary historians, Meacham asserts that white supremacy was the "cornerstone" of the founding of the Confederate States of America and that this bitter legacy continues to drive our polarized politics.

Meacham charts our long legacy of "partisan fury" over the centuries and details the cycles of progress and regress that have occurred throughout US history. Abraham Lincoln may have appealed to our "better angels," but his successor, Andrew Johnson, opposed granting citizenship to formerly enslaved African Americans. Lyndon Johnson worked with Martin Luther King Jr. to pass voting and civil rights legislation, yet racism continues to infect our social and economic systems.

Diversity trainer Robin DiAngelo puts it bluntly: "Today we [white Americans] have a cultural norm that insists we hide our racism from people of color and deny it among ourselves."[18] DiAngelo observes that rather than honestly acknowledging the reality of racism and white privilege, whites (and particularly white liberals) engage in myriad tactics to shield ourselves from the reality of the racist systems in which we are embedded and from which we benefit.

The legacy of enslavement and the reality of ongoing systemic racism produce profound racial inequities. According to the *Washington Post*, "white families have nearly 10 times the net worth of black families . . . and the gap is growing."[19] Further, while white families largely rebounded from the Great Recession by 2013, black and Hispanic families did not begin to see economic gains until four years later.[20] Despite these realities, as noted earlier a majority of whites believe they are in fact victims of discrimination.[21]

Research suggests that voters respond positively to grievance narratives when members of a disadvantaged minority are perceived to be unfairly "getting ahead." According to political scientist John Sides and colleagues, a sense of white vulnerability and of racial resentment were more important factors than economic anxiety among white millennials who voted for Donald Trump in 2016.[22]

Professor Glaude concludes that for many whites, the election of Barack Obama "signaled the end of entitlement for whites [and] occasioned a resurgence of white resentment that set the stage for Trump."[23] Professor Carol Anderson agrees: "The trigger for white rage, inevitably, is black advancement."[24] Paradoxically, those of us on the privileged end of the continuum of racial disparities appear to be the ones who are most driving the attendant polarization.

4. Sexism and Gender Inequality

Like racism, sexism and gender discrimination continue to infect American society. The most persistent evidence for gender discrimination is the wage differential between men and women. Although the gap has narrowed in the last forty years, most research concludes that women earn between 80 and 90 percent of what men earn in the same roles.[25]

However, do sexism and gender discrimination contribute to polarization? Public policy researcher Kathleen Geier points to economic inequality *among women* as a key determinant of support for the two major party candidates in 2016. She found a "yawning class divide" among white women voters, as college-educated (and generally higher-income) white female voters supported Clinton over Trump by 6 points, and their non–college educated (and generally lower-income) counterparts "chose Trump by a margin of 28 points."[26] Geier quotes Tamara Draut, a journalist who interviewed dozens of working-class women across the country: "They feel invisible in our politics, our economy and our culture."[27]

While there is a well-documented "gender gap" among American voters, as men are much more likely to vote Republican than are women, gender alone does not seem to be the prime contributor to polarization. The *class gap* between white college-educated women and white non–college educated women totaled 34 points in 2016—much larger than the 20-point *gender gap* overall.[28]

Yet, similar to white resentment, male resentment does seem to play a role in voting decisions. Dan Cassino, a political scientist at Fairleigh Dickinson University in Teaneck, New Jersey, suggests that threats to traditional masculinity affect male voting behavior. Cassino's research found that "the threat of losing the traditional norm of men as breadwinners led men to abandon support for the first major-party female candidate in American history and come out in support of her opponent."[29]

In summary, while class, race, and gender all matter in determining voting patterns, the most significant sociological contributors to polarization in the United States at this historical moment appear to be economic inequality and identity threat. When voters feel they are abandoned and bypassed, they are particularly vulnerable to populist and nationalist messages. Populism and nationalism both contribute to polarization, as they are predicated on "us vs. them" framing.

5. Differing Moral Universes

In addition to tribalism and identity threat, differing moral frameworks may be contributing to our polarized era. Ethics professor Jonathan Haidt suggests that "morality is the key to understanding humanity."[30] Haidt's essential premise is that we do not *think* our way to morality; we *intuit* it, and then use reasoning to explain our intuitive choice. For example, if my parents spanked me when I was growing up, I may intuit that spanking is an important aspect of parenting and develop a moral rationale that permits me to continue the practice with my own children.

According to Haidt, morality "binds and blinds," producing both significant group achievements and painful exclusion from the group. Because every human being exists simultaneously as an individual and as part of a larger society, we are subject to "parochial altruism."[31] Parochial altruism tends to produce generous and empathetic behaviors within a group but exclusionary or even violent behaviors with outsiders. The result can be a toxic tribalism or nationalism—a "my group, right or wrong" that excludes or harms others. However, it can also produce a group loyalty capable of extraordinary individual sacrifice, as we see among soldiers fighting together on the battlefield.

In Haidt's understanding, religion is not a *cause* of polarization but rather an *accessory* to the phenomenon. For example, some extremists who recruit suicide killers distort Islam to convince volunteers of the cosmic rewards of their mission. Closer to home, some Christian groups distribute voting guides indicating that God has a clear preference for certain candidates. In such cases, religion becomes a justification for the desired behavior, but is likely not the primary motivation.

Republican senator Ben Sasse of Nebraska offers a different explanation for our current state of division. In *Them: Why We Hate Each Other—and How to Heal*, Sasse suggests that the underlying cause is our lack of rootedness. "The real culprit," he writes, "has everything to do with us as uprooted, wandering souls."[32] Sasse charts the multiple upheavals that accompanied the information and technology revolution and concludes, "Community is collapsing, anxiety is building, and we're distracting ourselves with artificial political hatreds."[33] The solution, then, is to restore community, connection, and social capital (relationships).

For Sasse, the problem is rootlessness and disconnection, and the solution must therefore be rootedness and connection. For Haidt, the problem is blindness and exclusion, and the solution is the practice of empathy—particularly with outsiders.

6. Global Nationalism

When it comes to polarization, America is not exceptional. Populism and nationalism are also on the rise in Europe, Latin America, and parts of Asia and Africa—often confronting head-on the forces of globalism and open borders.[34] The great experiment in trans-European economic unity and political integration frayed with the Brexit vote in 2016. As with the economic factors influencing many American voters that year, "support for Brexit was associated with how well whites thought they were doing compared to minorities."[35]

In short, identity threat seems to be driving the rise in populism and nationalism around the world. One primary response to that threat is the growing worldwide pressure to limit immigration and to build walls.

British author Tim Marshall charts the primary reason for building walls—fear.[36] Whether designed to keep out the "barbarians" (ancient China), the immigrants (US and India), or the terrorists (Middle East), or to separate ethno-religious groups (Northern Ireland and Iraq), walls are generally built to reduce our anxieties. As genuine barriers, they often prove ineffective (just ask the Chinese). As symbols of protection and exclusion, however, walls are remarkably powerful.

Perhaps the most consistent aspect of inter-state wall building is that it tends to take place between poorer and richer countries. Marshall cites examples of walls between the United States and Mexico, Kuwait and Iraq, Saudi Arabia and Yemen, and India and Bangladesh. In all cases, the relatively richer country built the wall to keep out "intruders" from the relatively poorer country. Once again, we see that economic inequality is the driving force for the polarization symbolized by the erection of walls.

Marshall describes a "scenario familiar in countries across the world: fear and anger directed at immigrants, who are not only accused of taking local jobs but also of creating higher levels of crime by selling drugs, forming gangs and so on."[37] That such scapegoating occurs on every inhabited continent suggests that this is likely a human reaction that occurs when faced with threats to one's identity or economic status. Such threats produce fear, which in turn causes individuals and groups to "hunker down."

As in the 1930s, nationalism is on the rise across the globe. However, the underlying forces are economic inequality and identity threat. Walls represent artifacts of our economic inequality and our fears of foreigners. They are symptoms—not causes.

7. Balkanized Media

Numerous authors have identified the increasingly stratified media ("Fox News vs. MSNBC") and polarized social media as the cause of polarization. The days when most Americans got their news from a single source, such as Walter Cronkite of CBS News, are long gone. In the age of twenty-four-hour cable news networks and proliferating online news sources, the quest for viewers and clicks seems to drive the demand for conflict-generating stories. There also is clearly a media polarization industry that thrives on riling up listeners and viewers while taking regular breaks for "obscene profit timeouts."[38]

Yet there is substantial evidence that the proliferation of news sources *reflects* increasing polarization even more than it *contributes* to it. The primary evidence for this claim is the fact that social scientists have been tracking increasing polarization among the public since the early 1980s—well before Facebook, Twitter, and even Fox News were part of our daily lives (though CNN was founded in 1980). Second, the tendency of human beings to seek out evidence supporting their preexisting biases has been around for millennia. "Confirmation bias" is a well-established phenomenon that predates the rise of social media.[39]

Yet it is likely that the balkanized media and partisan internet sites are *reinforcing* our divisions. David Blankenhorn, founder of Better Angels, a citizens' organization that seeks to reduce political polarization in the United States,[40] suggests:

> Living in a media ghetto means less that my views are shaped and improved . . . than that they are hardened and made more extreme; what might've been analysis weakens into partisan talking points dispensed by identity-group leaders; moreover, because I'm exposed only to the most cartoonish, exaggerated versions of my opponents' views, I come to believe that those views are so unhinged and irrational as to be dangerous.[41]

In short, the balkanized media and partisan "news" sources are worsening our polarized situation and coarsening our discourse. For example, the ad hominem attacks (e.g., "Lyin' Ted" and "Little Marco") leveled by President Trump against his primary opponents in 2016 would have been unthinkable prior to the rise of talk radio, which normalized such discourse. As my colleague Lenore

Bajare-Dukes has written, "Decades of popular, right-leaning talk radio have established a style of discourse dominated by frustration and anger, skepticism of political elites and experts, scorn for liberals, and dismissal of alternative points of view."[42]

While few would disagree that polarized media and algorithmic bias[43] have worsened our divides, there is not sufficient evidence to conclude that either the balkanized media or social media *caused* our current polarized state. Rather, the balkanized media and fractured social media are electronic accelerators of the self-sorting that was already occurring among the body politic. I now have the option both to physically avoid my opinionated uncle at the family reunion and to unfriend him on Facebook. Either way, I am free from his troublesome opinions that might challenge my preexisting biases.

8. Political Structure

Perhaps the cause of modern polarization is our centuries-old "winner take all" political structure. Rather than establishing a parliamentary system that apportions representation based on the percentage of the vote obtained, the founders of the American republic designed a constitution that awards seats in Congress based purely on majority vote. Such a system, particularly given the rise of a two-party structure that the founders did not anticipate, may contribute to the polarization we are now experiencing.[44]

Political polarization did not suddenly appear in 2016. The phenomenon has been growing for decades and appeared in earlier epochs in the United States. In the 1950s, President Dwight Eisenhower espoused "the middle way" in his policies. As he wrote to a friend in 1954, "The critical problem of our time is to find and stay on the path that marks the way of logic between conflicting arguments advanced by extremists on both sides on almost every economic, political, and international problem that arises."[45]

According to political scientist Sam Rosenfeld, the parties' respective positions began to harden during the civil rights movement. As the Democratic Party at the national level endorsed the aims of the civil rights movement, many white southern Democrats felt increasingly alienated from their century-long embrace of the party. Republican strategists seized on the rift, as "Republican advocates of a coherent ideology for the party were disproportionally conservatives seeking formal alliances with southern whites."[46] The winner-take-all nature of the American political system enabled this strategy to turn nearly every southern state from Democratic to Republican.

An additional structural hypothesis is that partisan gerrymandering is the cause of the extreme polarization that we now see in Congress. The practice of drawing congressional boundaries to favor the election of a particular partisan candidate has been around for centuries but has become more sophisticated with the rise of software that permits fine-tuned data analysis. However, while gerrymandering likely contributes to polarization, there is little evidence that it is a major cause.[47] As with our polarized media, partisan gerrymandering may be more a *consequence* and an accelerator of polarization than a primary cause.

9. Social Sorting

While Congress was polarizing, so were American voters. Reporter Bill Bishop charts this development in *The Big Sort: Why the Clustering of Like-Minded America Is Tearing Us Apart.* Bishop demonstrates that after 1976, Republicans and Democrats grew more geographically segregated. According to Bishop, "The 1976 election between President Gerald Ford and Jimmy Carter took place at the time after World War II when Americans were most likely to live, work, or worship with people who supported a different political party."[48]

The problem is that growing homogeneity corresponds with increasing extremism, as individuals who participate in only like-minded groups tend to develop more extreme views. This phenomenon appears in the rise of white nationalism among young, working-class white men who form affinity groups online. While we might assume those with more education associate with a wider variety of people, the same homogenizing function occurs among the highly educated. According to Bishop, "the more educated Americans become—and the richer—the less likely they are to discuss politics with those who have different points of view."[49]

Bishop blames not gerrymandering but gentrification and other social trends for the increase in congressional districts primarily composed of like-minded people. "It doesn't appear that redistricting caused much, if any, of the increase in homogeneous districts," he writes.[50] As much as we would like to fault our political leaders and the media for the polarization we are now experiencing, it seems that social sorting is primarily a grass-roots phenomenon.

10. Leadership-Driven Polarization

We have arrived at the final proposed cause of our polarized era—leaders who foment polarization. Whether Hugo Chávez in Venezuela, Rodrigo Duterte in the Philippines, or Donald Trump in the United States, the most visible contributor to polarization is often deemed to be the person at the top of the polarized country.

Top political leaders occupy a paradoxical position. They are both contributors to and symbols of developments in their countries. Did presidents Chávez, Duterte, and Trump contribute to polarization in their countries? Each man demonized his enemies, attacked the press, and marginalized or expelled moderating voices within his government. Yet simultaneously, each man also became the most visible *symbol* of the profound polarization within his country. Leaders like Chávez, Duterte, and Trump are as much a *product of* as a *contributor to* the polarization over which they preside.

How do we know this? Countries do not elect highly polarizing leaders unless they are in a highly polarized, or desperate, state. Venezuelans elected Hugo Chávez during an economic crisis and at a time when there were huge disparities between the rich and the poor.[51] Filipinos elected Rodrigo Duterte in the midst of a wave of crime and corruption that they hoped he could stop.[52] In the United States, many Trump voters felt threatened and marginalized, fearing that they were losing their place in the country and wanting to "make American great again."[53]

Voters in Venezuela, the Philippines, and the United States were facing economic inequality and actual or perceived waves of crime and corruption, and many feared that they were losing out. All it took was a strongman to give voice to that fear and anxiety and thus win an election. What seems most likely is that highly polarizing leaders are able to capitalize on the identity and economic threats that a significant portion of the population is experiencing. *Threat* is therefore the necessary precondition, and *fear* is the mechanism that polarizing leaders employ to seize power.

In short, it took a combination of economic, social, and emotional factors to bring about the striking levels of political polarization we are now experiencing. Yet the rise of populism and nationalism would not have been possible without someone to give voice to the increasing marginalization and identity threat that many Americans were feeling. One formula that consistently produces a polarized society (or organization) is thus the following:

INCOME INEQUALITY +
IDENTITY THREAT +
ARTICULATED GRIEVANCE =
POLARIZATION

Leaders must pay attention to how these conditions are present not only on the national level but in their own communities. Recall that Bishop Sengulane in Mozambique would "listen to people at the church door" but also listen to his colleagues from other churches in the region and the country.

Prevention and Intervention

Is it possible to overcome the current level of polarization in US society and in other countries? I believe it is. Here are three possible ways we might attempt to do so. I will explore each of these, and additional options, in future chapters.

1. Change the Political Culture and Structure

Political scientists Thomas Mann and Norman Ornstein, authors of *It's Even Worse Than It Was*, propose ten remedies to change the US political culture.[54] With recommendations ranging from restoring "public shame" to implementing a variety of "local solutions," Mann and Ornstein conclude with a hopeful counterpoint to their otherwise depressing title. The authors believe that a "Westminster-style parliamentary system provides a much cleaner form of democratic accountability than the American system."[55] Unfortunately, there is little evidence of an appetite for such a dramatic structural change in a Congress that can barely pass an annual budget.

2. Change the Social/Religious Culture

Professor and Presbyterian minister James Calvin Davis believes that the route out of polarization lies through embracing paradox. "Perhaps tolerance and strong conviction are not mutually exclusive," Davis suggests.[56] Davis also believes that a shared faith focus will draw individuals together, noting that "sharing faith in God enables us to have faith in each other."[57] While the reality of a religiously pluralistic society may impede Davis's vision, his suggestions explicitly target people of faith.

3. Rebuild Civil Society

Yuval Levin, editor of the conservative journal *National Affairs*, offers a broader remedy. Levin agrees with Davis that we need to embrace paradox, specifically the "best of both stability and dynamism, diversity and cohesion, opportunity and prosperity."[58] In addition, Levin advocates for rebuilding the "mediating institutions" that occupy the middle ground between the individual and the state—family, community, and civil society. Levin views these traditional institutions as "counter-cultural agents of resistance" that offer alternatives to the domination of politics and the state.[59]

New York Times columnist Thomas Friedman, in his opinion piece "Where American Politics Can Still Work," proposes, "The country looks so much better from the bottom up." Friedman visits Lancaster, Pennsylvania, and observes a "complex adaptive coalition" of residents who are cooperating across political lines to improve the community. What is saving such communities, Friedman concludes, is "leadership without authority."[60] In short, the solution to societal polarization may be localism—cooperative efforts to improve our local communities.

Summary

Polarization is not a new phenomenon, nor is it limited to US society. It is, rather, a universal expression of human conflict that waxes and wanes over time. While the causes are multifaceted, societal polarization is most likely to arise in the presence of threats to an individual's or a group's identity or economic security. When demagogic leaders seize on ethno-religious differences to divide a group or society, polarization can become an extremely dangerous and potentially violent phenomenon.

Possible remedies for polarization include structural and cultural changes at the level of the broader society or the political system. While systemic reforms seem unlikely in the current dysfunctional political climate in the United States, I will argue that leaders at every level (family, community, organization) are well placed to be agents of reconnection in an age of polarization. Effective solutions to our current polarization will emerge community by community and organization by organization, and leaders will be required to elicit and enact such solutions.

Notes

1. Ben Bradlee Jr., *The Forgotten: How the People of One Pennsylvania County Elected Donald Trump and Changed America* (New York: Little Brown, 2018), 94.
2. Bradlee, *The Forgotten*, 87.
3. Drew Desilver, "For Most U.S. Workers, Real Wages Have Barely Budged in Decades," Pew Research Center, August 7, 2018, https://tinyurl.com/y2ok8x9z.
4. Chad Stone, Danilo Trisi, Arloc Sherman, and Roderick Taylor, "A Guide to Statistics on Historical Trends in Income Inequality," Center on Budget and Policy Priorities, August 29, 2018,

https://tinyurl.com/ycxhufef.

5. Robert Creamer, "To Reduce Political Polarization in Washington, We Must Reduce the Economic Polarization of America," Facts and Arts, January 11, 2010, https://tinyurl.com/y344najz.
6. Nolan McCarty, Keith T. Poole, and Howard Rosenthal, *Polarized America: The Dance of Ideology and Unequal Riches* (Cambridge, MA: MIT Press, 2016).
7. Hernan Winkler, "The Effect of Income Inequality on Political Polarization: Evidence from European Regions, 2002–2014," *Economics and Politics*, February 17, 2019, doi.org/10.1111/ecpo.12129.
8. Grace Donnelly, "Top CEOs Make More in Two Days Than an Average Employee Does in One Year," *Fortune*, July 20, 2017, https://tinyurl.com/y85vz6gn.
9. Sebastian Junger, *Tribe: On Homecoming and Belonging* (New York: Hachette Book Group, 2016), 3.
10. Lilliana Mason, *Uncivil Agreement: How Politics Became Our Identity* (Chicago: University of Chicago Press, 2018), 14.
11. Mason, *Uncivil Agreement*, 43.
12. Mason, *Uncivil Agreement*, 84.
13. Lenore Bajare-Dukes, "National Polarization: Description and Causes/Drivers" (unpublished, October 27, 2016).
14. Amy Chua, *Political Tribes: Group Instinct and the Fate of Nations* (New York: Penguin Press, 2018), 189.
15. Deborah Shmueli, Michael Elliott, and Sanda Kaufman, "Frame Changes and the Management of Intractable Conflicts," *Conflict Resolution Quarterly* 24, no. 2 (2006): 207–18.
16. Eddie S. Glaude Jr., "Our Racist Soul," *Time*, September 17, 2018, 42–45.
17. Jon Meacham, *The Soul of America: The Battle for Our Better Angels* (New York: Random House, 2018), 85.
18. Robin DiAngelo, *White Fragility: Why It's So Hard for White People to Talk about Racism* (Boston: Beacon, 2018), 50.
19. Tracey Jan, "White Families Have Nearly 10 Times the Wealth of Black Families. And the Gap Is Growing," *Washington Post*, September 28, 2017, https://tinyurl .com/y4ct72wr.
20. Jan, "White Families Have Nearly 10 Times the Wealth."
21. Don Gonyea, "Majority of White Americans Say They Believe Whites Face Discrimination," National Public Radio, October 24, 2017, https://tinyurl.com/y9n7jbw2.
22. John Sides, Michael Tesler, and Lynn Vavreck, *Identity Crisis: The 2016 Presidential Campaign and the Battle for the Meaning of America* (Princeton, NJ: Princeton University Press, 2018).
23. Glaude, "Our Racist Soul," 44.
24. Carol Anderson, *White Rage: The Unspoken Truth of Our Racial Divide*

(New York: Bloomsbury USA, 2017), quoted in DiAngelo, *White Fragility*, 96.

25. Nikki Graf, Anna Brown, and Eileen Patten, "The Narrowing, but Persistent, Gender Gap in Pay," Pew Research Center, April 9, 2018, https://tinyurl.com/y49w5sjg.
26. Kathleen Geier, "Inequality among Women Is Crucial to Understanding Hillary's Loss," *The Nation*, November 11, 2016, https://tinyurl.com/j3l6gag.
27. Geier, "Inequality among Women."
28. Danielle Paquette, "The Unexpected Voters behind the Largest Gender Gap in Recorded Election History," *Washington Post*, November 9, 2016, https://tinyurl .com/yyu7p8es.
29. Dan Cassino, "Emasculation, Conservatism, and the 2016 Election," *Context* 17, no. 1 (Winter 2018): 50.
30. Jonathan Haidt, *The Righteous Mind: Why Good People Are Divided by Politics and Religion* (New York: Vintage Books, 2012), 231.
31. Haidt, *The Righteous Mind*, 271.
32. Ben Sasse, *Them: Why We Hate Each Other—and How to Heal* (New York: St. Martin's, 2018), 15.
33. Sasse, *Them*, 236.
34. Steven Metz, "The Rise of Identity Populism Is Making the World More Dangerous," *World Politics Review*, November 2, 2018, https://tinyurl.com/y3svg3rt.
35. Sides, Tesler, and Vavreck, *Identity Crisis*, 216.
36. Tim Marshall, *Divided: Why We're Living in an Age of Walls* (London: Elliott & Thompson, 2018).
37. Marshall, *Divided*, 172.
38. This is the term Rush Limbaugh has used for his commercial breaks since 2008.
39. Wikipedia, s.v. "Confirmation Bias," November 21, 2018, https://tinyurl.com/78spc79.
40. "Our Story," Better Angels, January 2, 2019, https://tinyurl.com/yx9tzqm9.
41. David Blankenhorn, "The Top 14 Causes of Political Polarization," *The American Interest*, May 16, 2018, https://tinyurl.com/y883t4w7.
42. Bajare-Dukes, "National Polarization."
43. Wikipedia, s.v. "Algorithmic Bias," accessed May 27, 2019, https://tinyurl.com/y46qualg.
44. Ballotpedia, "Winner-Take-All Voting Methods," downloaded November 24, 2018, https://tinyurl.com/yxduv52x.
45. Sam Rosenfeld, *The Polarizers: Postwar Architects of Our Partisan Era* (Chicago: University of Chicago Press, 2018), 76.
46. Rosenfeld, *The Polarizers*, 59.

47. Fred Dews, "A Primer on Gerrymandering and Political Polarization," *Brookings Now*, Brookings Institution, July 6, 2017, https://tinyurl.com/yd62vtc2.
48. Bill Bishop, *The Big Sort: Why the Clustering of Like-Minded America Is Tearing Us Apart* (New York: Mariner Books, 2008), 9.
49. Bishop, *The Big Sort*, 286.
50. Bishop, *The Big Sort*, 30.
51. Michael Tarver, "Why Did Venezuelans Elect Hugo Chávez President?" History Hit Podcast with Michael Tarver, September 18, 2018, https://tinyurl.com/y3ofyusc.
52. Nash Jenkins, "Why Did the Philippines Just Elect a Guy Who Jokes about Rape as Its President?," *Time*, May 10, 2016, https://tinyurl.com/j4yc3ac.
53. Olga Khazan, "People Voted for Trump Because They Were Anxious, Not Poor," *The Atlantic*, April 23, 2018, https://tinyurl.com/y89uqrm9.
54. Thomas Mann and Norman Ornstein, *It's Even Worse Than It Was: How the American Constitutional System Collided with the New Politics of Extremism* (Philadelphia: Basic Books, 2012).
55. Mann and Ornstein, *It's Even Worse Than It Was*, 198.
56. James Calvin Davis, *Forbearance: A Theological Ethic for a Disagreeable Church* (Grand Rapids: Eerdmans, 2017), 87.
57. Davis, *Forbearance*, 101.
58. Yuval Levin, *The Fractured Republic: Renewing America's Social Contract in the Age of Individualism* (New York: Basic Books, 2016), 97.
59. Levin, *The Fractured Republic*, 157.
60. Thomas L. Friedman, "Where American Politics Can Still Work: From the Ground Up," *New York Times*, July 3, 2018, https://tinyurl.com/y72td8m2.

2

LEADERSHIP AND POLARIZATION

David R. Brubaker

> A real leader uses every issue, no matter how serious and sensitive, to ensure that at the end of the debate we should emerge stronger and more united than ever before.
>
> —Nelson Mandela

When Loren Swartzendruber became president of Eastern Mennonite University (EMU), Harrisonburg, Virginia, in January 2004, he learned that his predecessor had terminated a staff member for involvement in a same-sex relationship. As an institution embedded in the Mennonite Church, EMU adhered to the denomination's stance that marriage was reserved for one man and one woman and, thus, that employees with same-sex orientation must remain celibate. EMU's relationship with the Mennonite Church USA, and ongoing tension over inclusion of individuals with same-sex orientation in the church and its institutions, would accompany Swartzendruber's entire thirteen-year tenure.

Over time, EMU's students, faculty, and staff increasingly advocated for equal treatment of employees regardless of sexual orientation (including that LGBTQ faculty and staff members would also have the right to be in publicly recognized relationships). In 2009, students organized a group called "Safe Space" to provide "an open and loving space affirming people of all sexual orientations."[1]

In 2013, at the initiation of President Swartzendruber and with the support of his cabinet, EMU's board of trustees authorized a "Listening Process." The stated purpose was "to determine whether or not the hiring policy should be altered in regards to faculty and staff in covenanted same-sex relationships."[2] The process included twenty on-campus opportunities for students, faculty, and staff to engage in dialogue, as well as a written survey by which alumni, community members, and other external constituents could express their perspectives.

The Listening Process concluded in July 2015 with a formal board decision to change the hiring policy. However, both the decision itself and the process that produced it were conflictual. At a time when not only the Mennonite Church USA but multiple religious denominations around the country faced conflict over inclusion of LGBTQ individuals in the life and leadership of their congregations and institutions, EMU's very public process and President Swartzendruber's leading role in it became targets of ire from both ends of the spectrum.

Responses to the listening process pummeled Swartzendruber. "I would describe the experience as whiplash, as in one day I might have two conversations with people vociferously opposed to any change in the policy, and two conversations that it had to change and it had to change now,"[3] he shares.

Although the board of trustees ultimately changed the hiring policy so as to not discriminate on the basis of sexual orientation or gender identity, the process was costly for President Swartzendruber. "It definitely had a negative impact on me in terms of health," he reports. "You have to accept the fact that leadership is not about popularity. If you're on a big stage, you're going to have many people who hate your decisions . . . or at least disagree with you."

As he reflected on the process, Loren Swartzendruber reflected on the importance of being a nonanxious presence in the midst of great anxiety.

> Leading in an age of polarization means that we need to practice the art of nonanxious presence. . . . In the face of conflict we have a tendency to either leave the conflict or take on the anxiety, and neither of those options is good. The most successful leaders stay in the conflict, they don't run from it, but they refuse to take on the anxiety of the system.

Leading in an age of polarization can be head-spinning. Unlike in a non-polarized environment where a small minority feels strongly about a given issue, in a polarized context as much as two-thirds of a group may take polar opposite positions. (Cases of a group "splitting down the middle" may exist in anecdotes, but in nearly every polarized group about a third of its members are in the middle. Because they are less invested in the identified issue and often cowed by the intensity at the ends of the spectrum, we tend not to notice them as much.)

President Swartzendruber's experience of leading a process of change through a polarized minefield illustrates what leaders in many other organizations have endured as well. Having conducted multiple interventions in such contexts, I have noticed five features common to polarized environments:

1. **Personal Attacks.** The most persistent sign of a polarized environment is that leaders become the consistent targets of personal attacks ranging from disparaging the leader's character and integrity to actual physical assaults. Such attacks occur even when leaders scrupulously avoid taking a side in the polarized conflict, as they are then perceived by both sides as spineless and unprincipled.
2. **Holy War.** Language shifts when people polarize. Instead of talking about the "costs and benefits" of a given course of action, polarized individuals describe their conflicts in epic terms. It is a battle for the future of democracy, the survival of the organization, or a cosmic fight between good and evil. In a Level Five conflict (described in the introduction), the goal is generally to eliminate the "evil-doers" from the face of the earth.
3. **Distorted Information.** In a polarized conflict, information is used not to inform debate but to vanquish opponents. Therefore, polarized individuals will seek out information that supports their position, regardless of its veracity, and dismiss contradictory information. Information is weaponized in the cosmic struggle to vanquish evil. (Propaganda increases dramatically in wartime in every society, including democratic ones.[4])
4. **Relentless Obsession.** Polarized individuals maintain an obsessive focus on the issues that concern them and the individuals or groups they oppose. Because the stakes are seen as cosmically high, to relax in the struggle is to relent and, thus, to be vanquished. Organizational leaders in such an environment find themselves spending inordinate amounts of time addressing "the issues" related to the conflict—mainly because it's impossible to avoid them.
5. **Intractable Negotiations.** Given the personal attacks, distorted information, and cosmic consequences attached to "winning" or "losing," compromise becomes unthinkable and negotiating with the enemy is seen as reprehensible. Simple decisions, such as approving a budget to keep an

> organization running, are ensnared in the polarized dynamics and become yet another reason to distrust one's opponents.

Leading in such an environment requires a very different set of skills than what is described in the myriad leadership books that profess to "solve your leadership dilemmas." While thoughtful leaders normally want to plan a process, form a team, and work for consensus, patience with process and finding consensus will be elusive in a polarized environment. As President Swartzendruber observed, "In a polarized situation, people who have a strong opinion on either end of a given issue will often say to the leader, 'Process be damned!' You can't succumb to it, but the pressure is enormous."

As mentioned in the introduction, the twin temptations of leaders in a polarized context are either to take a side (fight) or to run from the fray (flee). But there is a third way beyond fight and flight for leaders caught in the web of polarized relationships. This path is well described by renowned leadership authors such as Brené Brown, John Maxwell, and Donna Hicks. It requires clarity, compassion, courage, and connection.[5] I will explore each of these in turn.

Clarity

Leaders who survive and even thrive in polarized environments demonstrate clarity at two levels—within themselves and with others. "Clear is kind. Unclear is unkind," according to author and professor Brené Brown.[6] What does it mean to have clarity within oneself? Most importantly, it requires that leaders know and act on their core values and principles. As President Swartzendruber reflected,

> Leaders in any environment, certainly in one that is polarized, have to begin with their own integrity. Parker Palmer talks about leading from the inside. Knowing myself internally, knowing what my values are, knowing what my vision is, my goals. I have to keep coming back to that . . . what are my values?

Every spring in an Organizational Behavior course I teach, I ask students to complete two instruments. The first is a personality assessment, known as the Friendly Style Profile, developed by psychologists Susan Gilmore and Patrick Fraleigh.[7] The second is a core values inventory based on the list of values from the Center for Ethical Leadership's Core Values instrument.[8] I then ask them to write a paper about how their personality style and core values shape their participation in organizations.

In the Friendly Style Profile, I score equally high in both Achieving/Directing and Affiliating/Perfecting in my "Calm" mode, but increase significantly in Achieving/Directing when under prolonged stress. That means I become less attentive to relationships and more task- and outcome-focused when in a "Storm." Knowing this, I have to remind myself to slow down and pay more attention to people and process when I am under stress, as that instinct does not come naturally.

Likewise, becoming explicit about my core values has enabled me to make conscious choices when faced with competing demands. Since my core values include "family" and "faith," I strive to schedule both time with family and weekly participation in my faith community. My other two core values are "justice" and "peace," so the pull to activism and conflict transformation is also very strong.[9]

What's important is that we know ourselves. The most destructive leaders I have encountered are those who were utterly clueless about their behavior and its impact on others. Doris Kearns Goodwin, the presidential historian and author, identifies a list of traits associated with effective leadership: "humility, acknowledging errors, shouldering blame and learning from mistakes, empathy, resilience, collaboration, connecting with people and controlling unproductive emotions."[10] All of these require self-awareness, as well as other-awareness.

Clarity within transfers to clarity with others. When we know who we are and what we believe, we naturally communicate that clarity to others. This is not an attempt to convert others to one's beliefs. Rather, it is an expression of candor or transparency—a willingness to reveal our inner thoughts and beliefs to others. "Daring leaders who live into their values are never silent about hard things," says Brown.[11]

During his four-decade career of consulting with congregations, Alban Institute senior consultant Speed Leas observed that two styles of leadership tended to get leaders into trouble in conflicted environments. The first was *authoritarianism*—a leader who insisted it was "my way or the highway" and further polarized the congregation through uncompromising positions. But the second, which caused just as many failed pastorates, was a completely *undefined* leadership style. These leaders refused to take a stand, insisting that "my opinion really doesn't matter." Congregants viewed this undefined leadership as unprincipled and manipulative, suspecting that such leaders really did have preferences but refused to reveal them.[12]

Clarity with others thus requires both internal clarity and relational courage—the willingness to reveal one's beliefs and values even at the risk of rejection or ridicule. Jesus demonstrated this clarity and courage in his inaugural sermon in his hometown of Nazareth, when he claimed a prophetic mantle and challenged the townsfolk to understand God in universal (rather than tribal) terms. The resulting uproar got him thrown out of town and nearly thrown off a cliff.[13]

Compassion

Leadership guru John Maxwell notes that "one of the greatest contributors to a polarized culture is the inability—or unwillingness—to think about the other person's point of view."[14] As with Jonathan Haidt's call for empathy,[15] compassion often requires us to contain our own convictions long enough to understand another's perspective.

Compassion and clarity belong together. Clarity compels us to speak with conviction. Compassion invites us to listen with concentration. It is in the dance between clarity and compassion that leaders build trust. We tend to respect leaders who know what they believe yet are equally interested in hearing about our beliefs and experiences.

Genuine compassion also requires that leaders be aware of the multiple sources of identity and life experiences that shape the radically different perspectives of human beings. Why would a laid-off miner in West Virginia not respond to promises to revive coal and restore mining jobs? Why would a woman who has been a victim of sexual harassment not be horrified by a presidential candidate bragging about his sexual exploits? We need to listen deeply and with compassion to understand the choices individuals make and the beliefs they adopt.

Compassion does not require agreement. Compassion requires that I acknowledge the dignity of another human being and commit to attempting to understand their perspective. This very attempt creates a human bond that may overcome polarization. In the words of Nelson Mandela, "Our human compassion binds us the one to the other—not in pity or patronizingly, but as human beings who have learnt how to turn our common suffering into hope for the future."[16]

Courage

Brené Brown writes that she defines a leader as "anyone who takes responsibility for finding the potential in people and processes, and who has the courage to develop that potential."[17] Polarized times demand courageous leadership—in universities, businesses, congregations, nonprofit organizations, and government.

Loren Swartzendruber's story illustrates the courage required to initiate a listening and change process on a highly polarized issue within a university. President Swartzendruber chose to undertake this challenge as he approached retirement. "It was easier for me to lead the process at the end of my career [than it would have been earlier on] for two reasons. One, I wasn't looking for another position, and, two, I had experience with which to weather the storm." Still, the struggle was costly in terms of relationships. "I did lose relationships. There are people who were supporters of mine who no longer are. I had to remind myself that as a leader you are rarely as bad as your biggest critics think you are. Neither are you as great as your biggest fans think you are!" Courage may require risking one's reputation and relationships.

Business leaders in the United States operate within the same polarized environment as do other organizational leaders. Business leaders are regularly faced with questions about how to lead in a polarized age. Do they permit employees to have partisan political paraphernalia in the workplace? Do they sign a petition urging that local school board members vote "Yes" on funding for a new high school? Courage may also demand that business leaders make decisions based on the needs of their communities and societies—not just based on the quarterly report.

Congregational leaders face particular challenges, as a congregation is one of the few venues in American society where individual members still expect to exercise voice and participate in governance. Because congregations are also seen as sites of moral discernment, issues swirling in the broader society inevitably find their way into our sanctuaries and fellowship halls. In recent generations, congregations have conversed and convulsed over women in leadership, LGBTQ participation, abortion, war and peace, racism, sexual abuse, and more. Courage may prod congregational leaders to take a stand on issues for which consensus is elusive.

Leaders of other not-for-profit organizations also swim in a polarized cultural sea. The very nature of their mission may require them to advocate for individuals whose identities (as immigrants, prisoners, LGBTQ, impoverished, etc.) have become entangled in the country's culture wars. And many not-for-profit organizations receive grants or contracts from large foundations or government agencies that are, themselves, deeply embedded in one end or the other of the polarized spectrum. Courage may mean that nonprofit leaders speak out alongside those who have been marginalized.

Finally, leaders in government may face the toughest challenge, as governing at all levels (local, state or provincial, and national) has suffered most from the increasing incivility that accompanies polarization. Whether in town halls or on social media, government leaders are likely to be blasted by those who are unhappy with their decisions. Finding sufficient common ground to make major public-policy decisions becomes nearly impossible when legislatures are narrowly divided. Courage may compel a politician to reach across the aisle to find agreement with a hostile adversary.

Connection

Leaders who survive and thrive in polarized environments exhibit clarity, compassion, courage, and connection. Such leaders begin with an internal connection to their own values, beliefs, and emotions. They are then able to connect with those they lead and with the communities in which they live and work. Finally, they strive to stay connected even with their enemies. Staying connected with our enemies requires an acknowledgment that they, too, possess basic dignity.

The capacity to recognize the inherent dignity of others, and particularly of those with whom we profoundly disagree, may be the most crucial attribute of leaders who succeed in polarized times. We will start to overcome polarization when we commit to respecting the fundamental dignity of every human being. Harvard professor Donna Hicks, who has done pioneering work on the importance of dignity, describes the three connections that define dignity as (1) connection to our *own* dignity, (2) connection to the dignity of *others*, and (3) connection to the dignity of something *larger* than ourselves.[18]

Leaders must first embrace their own inherent dignity. Hicks distinguishes between respect, which must be earned, and dignity, which is inherent. In my own belief system, I see every human being as a beloved child of God and, thus, possessing inherent dignity. For those of a humanist bent, inherent dignity resides within every person simply because they are human.

Perhaps no president in American history demonstrated connection and dignity as did Abraham Lincoln. In historian Doris Kearns Goodwin's masterful *Leadership in Turbulent Times*, she profiles Lincoln, along with Lyndon Johnson, Theodore Roosevelt, and Franklin Roosevelt.[19] Goodwin describes Lincoln as convinced that "if slavery is not wrong, nothing is wrong."[20] But she also details his emotional intelligence, "his empathy, humility, consistency, self-awareness, self-discipline, and generosity of spirit."[21]

Lincoln's commitment to staying connected with his deepest

principles, his friends, and his enemies—along with his embrace of the dignity of every person—ultimately led his Cabinet to support the Emancipation Proclamation and the Union to embrace it. Goodwin concludes, "In a great convergence of the man and the times, Abraham Lincoln's leadership imprinted a moral purpose and meaning on the protracted misery of the Civil War."[22]

Building Community Connections

For most leaders, the connections that matter most are the ones we make in our own communities. Rev. Jennifer Davis Sensenig became the lead pastor of Community Mennonite Church (CMC) in Harrisonburg, Virginia, in 2008. CMC is a medium-sized congregation of about three hundred active members, and is known for its participatory internal governance and external engagement with the broader community. Over the years the congregation has incubated a variety of nonprofit organizations, as well as provided a weekly food pantry for community members facing food insecurity.

As a member of the local Interfaith Association, CMC also helped launch "Open Doors," which offers shelter for neighbors without safe shelter during the cold months (November through March) in Harrisonburg and the surrounding county. Open Doors functions by rotating the sheltering function among some twenty area congregations (Christian, Jewish, and Muslim) that each host the homeless residents for a week. As Open Doors was reaching capacity, Rev. Davis Sensenig and several lay leaders agreed on the need to do more to address the structural causes of homelessness, including the lack of affordable housing. They started with networking, as she shares:

> We began with lots of local meetings with Open Doors, with advocates who were homeless themselves, with individuals who cared about unsheltered neighbors, with United Way, the Community Services Board, and the Housing Authority. When we were frustrated, getting nowhere, we explored congregation-based community organizing, which led us to take a field trip to experience an organization called IMPACT in Charlottesville, Virginia.[23]

IMPACT is composed of member congregations working to address the root causes of various problems in Charlottesville. IMPACT's mission is to "empower the faith community of greater Charlottesville to create significant social change through unified direct action."[24] Pastor Davis Sensenig was moved when she participated in an IMPACT meeting of over 1,000 people that featured reports on successful efforts to address local homelessness through rapid rehousing measures and permanent supportive housing.

Rev. Davis Sensenig and a few other faith leaders worked to organize a similar coalition of congregations, ultimately dubbed "Faith in Action," in Harrisonburg and Rockingham County. She explains their launch strategy:

> We did direct mailings and spoke about Faith in Action at Interfaith gatherings. We had events where we invited pastors, bought them lunch, and talked about our vision. A big part of organizing was talking to congregations about the difference between ministries of compassion or service and justice work. Justice ministry requires that congregations work together across our differences. No single congregation can take on these big issues by themselves.

As of 2019, Faith in Action consists of twenty-four member congregations—including the local mosque, synagogue, and Unitarian Universalist Association, and twenty-one Christian congregations ranging from conservative to progressive. After a listening campaign among the congregations and their related ministries, Faith in Action identified, through a participatory process, its top issue to confront: "local justice for our immigrant neighbors." One significant outcome of that effort was a decision by Harrisonburg's City Council to formally join the "Welcoming America" network of communities that welcome immigrants.[25] Pastor Sensenig observed that the effort "increased our integrity, as we were listening to our immigrant neighbors."

As of this writing, Faith in Action is addressing criminal justice reform at both the city and county levels. Through its "Issues Committee," the organization drafted three "asks" that included creating a new position, Community Justice Planner, for the city of Harrisonburg.[26] According to Pastor Davis Sensenig, "It's a bit too early to know how the current effort will turn out, but at least it's being talked about. I think we're changing the conversation." Changing the conversation, as well as who participates in the conversation, is one of the most significant achievements of Faith in Action.

By bringing together twenty-four very diverse congregations to work collectively on deeply rooted systemic issues, Faith in Action is also reducing polarization among member congregations and within the broader community. Pastor Davis Sensenig identifies *partnerships* and *persistence* as key to making progress:

> Our strength is our faith and our congregations, but in both of these campaigns we've developed significant partnerships with other organizations, for example the Valley Justice Coalition. The Northeast Neighborhood Association (a historically African American neighborhood) is another significant partner. We've had conflicts with every partner, but we've been able to work with one another. This work takes persistence if you want to make progress. Building partnerships takes time, but they are essential. Persistence is really about what you're going to do when people say no.

Rev. Davis Sensenig understands that building and sustaining partnerships is primarily about building and maintaining relationships. She cites shared values, a common focus, and interpersonal relationships as the triad that holds Faith in Action together. With this solid base, Faith in Action has been able to span multiple faiths, diverse Christian traditions, and even the rural–urban divide that isolates Democratic Harrisonburg from surrounding Republican Rockingham County. Pastor Davis Sensenig is clearly motivated by her faith as a follower of Jesus, and she credits her faith with sharpening her strategic instincts:

> Among Christian congregations and denominations, we can contribute to another way of relating to neighbors. Unless we have a structural way of doing that, it doesn't seem to happen. From the very beginning we recognized that our congregations are already made up of both city and county residents. We are going to cross that cultural divide intentionally.

Given that Pastor Davis Sensenig is both the lead pastor of a growing congregation and president of Faith in Action, an observer might wonder what she does to sustain herself. Her answer reflects an ongoing commitment to daily, weekly, monthly, and annual rituals:

> I get up in the morning and I pray and exercise. I take a Sabbath Day every week, on Fridays, and a weeklong spiritual retreat every year. I take a prayer and planning day once a month. I walk and ride my bike to work.

Leading systemic change efforts in an era of polarization requires both coalition-building and an unwavering commitment to self-care.

Leadership Counsel

Few individuals are eager to lead in a polarized time. Yet leaders today cannot escape this reality. How, then, should we lead? Following are five suggestions from my own observations of successful leaders in polarized contexts:

Engage Conflict When It Emerges, Not Just after It Erupts

As conflict emerges in an organization or other system, conflict-savvy leaders move toward it when it's small, rather than avoid it and allow the conflict to grow larger. They do this in two ways. First, they *invite disagreement* by encouraging members of the system to come to them directly when they have a concern. Second, such leaders take the initiative to *approach others*, rather than avoid them, when they sense a strained relationship, and encourage others to do the same. These leaders model direct engagement and encourage others to do likewise.

I know a minister in a large congregation in the southern United States who practices this principle. If he hears "through the grapevine" that someone has concerns about his ministry or the direction of the congregation, he invites the person to have coffee or lunch in a neutral location. In the course of the conversation, the minister encourages the person to share their hopes and concerns for the congregation. Opening the door in this way generally releases the concerns in a context where both parties can have a relaxed conversation. Such direct engagement tends to defuse resentment that otherwise might fester and grow.

Learn to "Manage Polarities," Not Just "Resolve Conflicts"

When a system polarizes, it's often because the two ends of the spectrum are unable to hold together competing truths or realities. A classic example is the ongoing battle between those who advocate for "individual freedom" and those who call for "community responsibility." These are essentially expressions of the fundamental human needs for both autonomy and affiliation. As consultant and author Barry Johnson suggests, the challenge is not to "resolve the conflict" between these two perspectives but to "manage the polarities" that exist within the system.[27]

In my experience, the group that is often best able to live with polarities lies in the "critical middle"—those individuals in the system who embrace both ends of this artificial dichotomy and are able to receive the "truth" that each end of the spectrum is advancing. Even in a highly polarized environment, there will be a significant-sized group in the middle. The challenge for leaders is to provide mechanisms for others in the organization to also hear their voices.

Remember That as Goes the Leadership, So Goes the Organization

After more than three decades of consulting with congregations and other religious organizations, I can now predict, with about 90 percent accuracy, which systems will "split" and which will "stay together" when confronted with high-level conflict. If those in leadership—both formal and informal—are able to remain in a respectful coexistence, the likelihood of a genuine schism is remarkably low. However, if the leadership group itself polarizes and then splits, the system will almost always do likewise. "A house divided against itself cannot stand"—and particularly when the "parental" figures model toxic conflict behaviors.

Three of the most destructive conflict behaviors are avoidance, belligerence, and contempt. While temporary withdrawal from a conflict situation can be constructive, chronic avoidance generally leads to relational deterioration. Belligerence from one party tends to escalate conflict and to invite hostility from the other party in return. And contempt may be the most destructive conflict behavior, whether in a marriage or in a work relationship.[28] By contrast, the three most constructive conflict behaviors are the opposite of toxic behaviors. Rather than avoidance, belligerence, and contempt, they are engagement, openness, and respect. When we choose to engage an adversary with openness and respect, we can transform the relationship.

Speak Your Truth

As Speed Leas observed, leaders who decline to self-define can be as frustrating to followers as autocratic leaders. This doesn't mean that leaders must speak out on every controversial issue, as every wise leader must choose their battles. But it does suggest that effective leadership in a polarized environment will sometimes require a leader to take a stand. This is when moral clarity, informed by one's core values, becomes the North Star for leaders, guiding them to a principled, rather than a reactive, stance.

Nelson Mandela is often described as an exemplar of moral clarity, both in his unflinching opposition to apartheid in South Africa and in his unwavering commitment to racial reconciliation after his release from twenty-seven years in prison. When we combine respectful engagement with moral clarity, we release a powerful leadership force that can transform even highly polarized relationships.

Protect Your People

Perhaps the most important function of leaders is to safeguard the people who work or worship in their organizations and congregations. As Simon Sinek says in *Leaders Eat Last,* "The true price of leadership is the willingness to place the needs of others above your own."[29] Employees and congregants instinctively sense whether a leader is focused on the needs of others or primarily concerned about their own advancement. Sinek calls on leaders to see their responsibility as protecting their people and creating a "circle of safety" inside their organizations.

Such a circle of safety is critically important in a polarized environment. Given the dehumanizing discourse and even physical threats that accompany polarization, organizational members inevitably look to leaders to provide calm and safety. The worst leaders will pile on—accelerating the division and fear already present in the environment. The best leaders will take a stand—creating a circle of safety for members in the midst of the storm.

We live in an increasingly polarized (and anxious) age. But those in leadership roles, at whatever level, have great influence over how their systems experience the broader societal polarization. If they can engage conflict, manage polarities, commit to respectful cooperation, speak truth, and protect their people, the likelihood of internal conflict reaching Level Four or Five is significantly reduced. And if conflict does reach those higher levels, the losses that are experienced will be minimized.

The skills of engaging conflict, managing polarities, cooperating respectfully, speaking truth, and protecting people can be learned. The deeper reality is that exercising these skills, particularly in high-intensity conflict, requires significant emotional and spiritual maturity. How can leaders develop such maturity? Here, the insights of Family Systems Theory, particularly as interpreted by Dr. Edwin Friedman for organizational leaders, are essential. Leaders who learn to self-define while staying connected are the most likely to successfully employ these strategies.[30]

To "self-define" means to develop the internal and external clarity that we discussed earlier in this chapter. To stay connected implies that we refuse to cut off relationships with those we disagree with (unless such relationships have become abusive). This paradoxical ability–to clearly define oneself while also welcoming others' self-definition, lies at the heart of successfully leading in an age of polarization.

As leaders, we can choose to manage our polarities on the basis of our deepest beliefs and values, including the importance of staying connected. In the next chapter we will explore how to communicate in a divided age.

Notes

1. "EMU's Diversity Timeline," Eastern Mennonite University, accessed January 5, 2019, https://tinyurl.com/y4zz2njt.
2. "EMU's Diversity Timeline."
3. All quotes from Loren Swartzendruber in this chapter are from an interview conducted by Lenore Bajare-Dukes on September 22, 2016.
4. Wikipedia, s.v. "American Propaganda during World War II," accessed May 27, 2019, https://tinyurl.com/ycn8wtpz.
5. John Maxwell, "Leading in Polarized Times," JohnMaxwell.com blog, November 13, 2018, https://tinyurl.com/y3vn9fxx. Maxwell adds a fifth "C," "candor," which I'm incorporating under "clarity."
6. Brené Brown, *Dare to Lead: Daring Greatly and Rising Strong at Work* (New York: Random House, 2018), 44.
7. Susan Gilmore and Patrick Fraleigh, *The Friendly Style Profile for People at Work* (Eugene, OR: Friendly Press, 2004), https://tinyurl.com/yc22cd5t.
8. "Self-Guided Core Values Assessment," Center for Ethical Leadership, 2002, https://tinyurl.com/zz5p3q6.
9. The Center for Ethical Leadership encourages readers to settle on just two core values, and if pressed, I would prioritize "faith" and "justice." The reason? My faith includes a commitment to family, and I believe that genuine peace is only possible with justice.
10. James B. Stewart, "Why Trump's Unusual Leadership Style Isn't Working in the White House," *New York Times*, January 10, 2019, https://tinyurl.com/y8emh4jd.
11. Brown, *Dare to Lead*, 184.
12. From "Consulting with Highly Conflicted Churches," an Alban Institute workshop led by Speed B. Leas and attended by the author in January 1989.
13. The story is recorded in Luke 4:14–30.
14. Maxwell, "Leading in Polarized Times."
15. Jonathan Haidt, *The Righteous Mind: Why Good People Are Divided by Politics and Religion* (New York: Vintage Books, 2012), 231.
16. Nelson Mandela Foundation, "Message by Nelson Mandela at Healing and Reconciliation Service Dedicated to HIV/AIDS Sufferers and 'The Healing of Our Land,' Johannesburg," December 6, 2000, https://tinyurl.com/ybkjuv2e.

17. Brown, *Dare to Lead*, 4.
18. Donna Hicks, *Leading with Dignity: How to Create a Culture That Brings Out the Best in People* (New Haven: Yale University Press, 2018).
19. Doris Kearns Goodwin, *Leadership in Turbulent Times* (New York: Simon & Schuster, 2018).
20. Goodwin, *Leadership in Turbulent Times*, 17.
21. Goodwin, *Leadership in Turbulent Times*, 222–23.
22. Goodwin, *Leadership in Turbulent Times*, 242.
23. All quotes from Jennifer Davis Sensenig are taken from an interview with the author conducted on February 7, 2019.
24. "About IMPACT: Interfaith Movement Promoting Action by Congregations Together," accessed February 8, 2019, www.impactcville.com.
25. Holly Stauffer, "Harrisonburg City Council Passes 'Welcome America' Resolution by Faith in Action," WHSV, August 24, 2016, https://tinyurl.com/y3huv6py.
26. The other two "asks" put forward by Faith in Action are (1) eliminating the daily "keep fees" charged to families of the incarcerated at the downtown and regional jails, and (2) increasing restorative justice opportunities for juveniles.
27. Barry Johnson, *Polarity Management: Identifying and Solving Unsolvable Problems* (Amherst, MA: HRD Press, 2014).
28. Ellie Lisitsa, "The Four Horsemen: Criticism, Contempt, Defensiveness, and Stonewalling," The Gottman Institute, April 23, 2013, https://tinyurl.com/jfnk7xf.
29. Simon Sinek, *Leaders Eat Last: Why Some Teams Pull Together and Others Don't* (New York: Portfolio/Penguin, 2017), xii.
30. David Cox, "The Edwin Friedman Model of Family Systems Thinking," *Academic Leadership: The Online Journal* 4, no. 4 (Fall 2006).

3

COMMUNICATING ACROSS THE DIVIDE

Everett N. Brubaker

> Language is not a neutral medium. It does not simply reflect a reality that is "out there." From birth, the social worlds we inhabit are structured through language. For that reason, we see the world and understand our experiences through the symbols, meanings, and social categories that we have learned and developed. They are our lenses: we have no way of understanding things other than through the meaning structures built through language in our environments.
>
> —Oliver Escobar

It's the night of the 2016 election. While the country anxiously watches the votes come in that will decide the next president of the United States, a coalition of activists in Florida gather in a room at a local restaurant to watch a different set of votes. While eager to see the presidential results themselves, this coalition had their eye specifically on a ballot referendum they had just spent months fighting against. Amendment 1, while masquerading as a pro-solar amendment, aimed to increase the state energy monopoly's control on solar, while simultaneously limiting the ability for customers to own and sell their own solar energy.

The coalition at the restaurant, Floridians for Solar Choice, was supported by the usual, politically left-leaning environmental "suspects" (350.org, Greenpeace USA, Sierra Club Florida, etc.). However, this coalition was actually founded by a somewhat peculiar mix of not-so-typical, politically right-leaning organizations including Conservatives for Energy Freedom, the Republican Liberty Caucus of Florida, and Christian Coalition of America, to name a few. As you might imagine, the scene unfolding at the restaurant was an interesting one: two sides, those pulling for Hillary Clinton and those wanting Donald Trump, watching the results roll in together; each rooting for dramatically different presidential outcomes, while together eagerly hoping Amendment 1 does not pass.

According to Debbie Dooley, at the restaurant the night of the election, each side stayed mostly in their own corner. But when the results came in that the ballot referendum did not pass, "we all came together in the middle of the room and toasted with a glass of champagne!" Dooley continued, "And then we just went to separate rooms. When you're working with a bipartisan coalition, you don't talk about your differences; you focus on what you have in common."[1]

Debbie Dooley doesn't fit the profile typical of an environmental activist: cofounder of the Tea Party, free market champion, gun rights supporter, and advocate of other decidedly conservative stances. Yet Dooley has been a solar activist for nearly a decade and is founder of the Green Tea Coalition, a partnership between the Sierra Club (Green) and the Tea Party (Tea) to fight Georgia Power and to advocate for green energy. She is known nationally for bridging the political divide on renewables, driving pro-solar messages that the political right can get excited about.

How is it that Republicans and Democrats came together so successfully in support of solar energy in Florida? Dooley cites their specific common goal (to keep Amendment 1 from passing) as well as the ability of the groups to focus on the "20 percent we agree on." However, the key for this bipartisan coalition was how strategically, thoughtfully, and effectively they communicated, both internally among coalition members and externally with members of the public.

Not only can examining our language and the ways we communicate help us understand a key source of our polarization, but it can also offer tools to help address this national challenge. This chapter first outlines the importance of understanding the power of language itself: How does our language reflect our polarized context? And how does our language actually create (constitute) and reproduce our polarized context? I then propose how leaders can begin to practice mindfulness in their language to help depolarize our communication.

In light of how Dooley and other leaders of politically conservative environmental groups communicate with conservative (and liberal) audiences about climate change and environmental issues, I then explore the importance of three components in any communication event: the message, the messenger, and the audience. With profound polarization around a variety of issues in our country, bridging the political divide is fundamental to the health, security, and sustainability of our democracy. Finally, I will suggest how leaders can move toward more mindful communication and how the deliberative dialogue movement can aid in addressing our intensely polarized society.

The Power of Language

The language we speak is a powerful mediator of how we understand and describe our world. Research on the power of language has progressed since the dramatic claims of Benjamin Lee Whorf in the 1940s. His original assertion claimed that language actually *determines* what we can think about, that we are "imprisoned" by our language. For Whorf, if one did not have the language for an experience or concept, then there was no way that person or culture could understand ("think") that particular phenomenon. However, Whorf's absolutist assertion has been largely challenged by modern linguists.[2] While recent linguistic research has explored the way different languages *influence* how we think about such things as gender,[3] memory,[4] and space,[5] research has largely refuted the deterministic assertion of Whorf that an individual is unable to conceptualize a phenomenon because they do not have a word for it in their language.

The degree to which language directs our reality is still negotiated among linguists and others. However, the power of language to influence how we move through the world is widely accepted. Northern Illinois University professor Betty Birner of the Linguistic Society of America (LSA) summarizes this idea:

> The influence of language isn't so much on what we can think about, or even what we do think about, but rather on how we break up reality into categories and label them. And in this, our language and our thoughts are probably both greatly influenced by our culture.[6]

So how might this understanding of the relationship between language and culture inform our conversations surrounding polarization and leadership? First, it is helpful to acknowledge that the English language generally leans toward binaries, lacking significant words to describe experiences, feelings, or events that occupy "the middle." Second, while political polarization is not a new phenomenon, it has been posited that the polarization of our political *language* largely is.[7] This new polarized language has led to the use of completely different words or phrases to describe commonly observed phenomena (e.g., "illegal alien," "asylum seeker," "undocumented worker"). This polarized language can help us understand why at times it feels like our politically differing neighbor or family member speaks an entirely different language or operates in what seems an entirely different reality.

When I teach undergraduate first-year students about language, I lead them through an activity demonstrating the binary nature of our language. First, I ask the students to think of the antonym for a dozen or so words they see on a screen. For example, when they see the word "old," they generally write "young"; if they see the word "wrong," they usually offer the word "right." After they create these opposite pairs, I ask them to go back and write a word that captures what the "middle" would be—that is, the "in-between" of the two words they have written. This usually takes students a much longer time, and often the words they select aren't specific enough to capture what they intend. Words like "average," "medium," and "middle" are used and reused to capture the center of a variety of experiences and feelings. (If I'm between *right* and *wrong,* am I . . . *kind of right? Average?*)

In many instances, we simply do not have the words to describe the middle, the in-between, or the nuance of a particular situation, experience, or event. Introductory communication textbooks thus often describe "polarization" as "the use of either-or language that causes us to perceive and speak about the world in extremes."[8] This "word opposites" activity sets the stage for unpacking how language might influence political polarization and conflict more broadly.

Outside the classroom, our tendency toward binaries can be seen in our political discourse. While voters' beliefs and positions on various issues are often a bit muddy and complicated, pollsters, politicians, and neighbors often ask about a person's stance in a binary: pro-life or pro-choice, for legalization of "x" or against, with this movement or counter to it, and so forth. In a 2018 *Atlantic* piece, political journalist Conor Friedersdorf argues that voters might recognize they have a lot more in common if issues were framed along spectrums. In between "pro-life" and "pro-choice," Friedersdorf argues, sits "a staggering array of coherently distinguishable positions."[9] Moving away from binaries, he argues, helps reveal instances when "differences between Americans are not as sharp as they might seem, and enable marginal improvements to policy on issues where slippery slopes are unlikely and the main obstacle holding back reform is the fear of a limit that almost no one wants to cross."[10]

Friedersdorf offers the example of immigration policy, where Democrats often articulate a firm policy in terms of openness (e.g., Dreamer policy) and Republicans articulate a firm policy in terms of limits (e.g., deportation or border wall), mainly to appease their respective bases. Yet despite their rhetoric, it is unlikely that most Democrats actually want a truly open border, or that most Republicans believe every illegal immigrant should be deported, or that either group sees Dreamer policy or limits on immigration as slippery slopes to open or closed borders. The emphasis on binaries thus prevents sensible efforts at bipartisan policy that would likely be supported by the electorate.

Binaries in popular discourse take many forms: false dichotomies, either/or framing, black-and-white discourse, all-or-nothing language, and more. Each of these forms captures the reality that the language we use favors polarization. An awareness, or mindfulness, of this tendency is key to addressing polarization. However, what happens when the language we use doesn't even seem to be on the same spectrum as that of our political counterparts? In these cases, it doesn't seem that our two "languages" are on either end of a spectrum, but on different spectrums entirely.

Communication professor Dietram Scheufele from the University of Wisconsin articulates this phenomenon. Quoted in a 2017 *Business Insider* article, Scheufele claims, "Every tribe has its own words . . . and it becomes more and more difficult to have conversations across tribal fault lines if we can't even agree on the terminology."[11] Today's phrases and bumper sticker–style arguments are jam-packed with wildly different meanings and assumptions. When arguments pull deeply from each side's own lexicon (their group's suite of vocabulary), it becomes nearly impossible to hold a conversation, let alone reach a decision or agreement.

One of the most interesting studies to highlight this phenomenon comes from researchers at Stanford and Brown Universities. While acknowledging that political polarization is not a new phenomenon, their analysis of congressional speeches from 1873 to 2009 finds that polarized *language* is "a striking exception."[12] They summarize:

> Democrats and Republicans now speak different languages to a far greater degree than ever before. The fact that partisan language diffuses widely through media and public discourse

> implies that this could be true not only for congresspeople but for the American electorate more broadly.

Their study found that, as we approached the turn of the century, an individual's ability to guess the political party of a congressperson based solely on the language they used increased. Using a unique algorithm,[13] the researchers found that someone reading a congressional address over the one hundred–plus years from 1873 to the early 1990s consistently had around a 55 percent chance of correctly guessing political party based on the language used. After 1994, however, that percentage jumps to around 83 percent. These findings have huge implications for leaders' communication. The words we choose matter. Terms and phrases we might assume simply *describe* a phenomenon are loaded with differing political meanings. This finding echoes Escobar's clarifying words at the chapter's opening: "Language is not a neutral medium."

Toward a Mindfulness of Language

My intent in unpacking the influence and power of our language is not to invite paralysis, but to encourage mindfulness. If we know our language favors polarity and has led to entirely different ways of speaking about an issue, it is critical that we be intentional about the words we use and mindful of their potential impact. First, one simple way to depolarize our language is to use language that describes or reflects spectrums rather than sides. Explore nuance, even when it doesn't seem like we have the words to do so. Avoid binaries and be careful with reductionisms (reducing a complex issue to an oversimplified statement). Utilize language that expands understanding of a topic or demographic. Since much of our communication is driven by ritual (when was the last time you *actually* told someone how you were feeling when they asked you how you were?), mindfulness is key to avoiding language that favors sides, slogans, and secondhand discourse.[14]

Second, it is critical that we use words that are grounded and unpacked. Most words won't require this. A door is a door to most people. While the images we conjure in our heads might be slightly different, the overall meaning and purpose of *door* is generally shared. Predictably, words that are more abstract, like *freedom*, often demand a bit more analysis. One helpful way to think about the differing levels of abstraction of our words is to consider two purposes, or functions, of language—an understanding influenced by the work of Russian linguist Roman Jakobson.[15] Language is used to describe, or reference,[16] everyday objects and experiences (like a door). Additionally, a unique function of language is its ability to describe itself[17] as well as things that aren't present or material (like freedom). As we move up this "ladder"[18] of abstraction, the words we use suddenly become less concrete, holding more and different meanings. This is not to say these more abstract words or phrases are off limits, but simply to encourage mindfulness in their use. I know for a fact that my conservative friends and I have very different understandings of what is involved when one talks about "freedom" or "national security." Taking the time (and sometimes exercising the self-restraint) to understand their definitions and explain my own opens up surprising avenues toward common ground.

Case Study: Politically Conservative Environmental Communication

To further explore ways to communicate across politically polarized divides, let's look to one of the most polarizing issues of the twenty-first century: global climate change and environmental policy. Despite bipartisan efforts in the 1970s to implement a host of federal environmental protection policies, modern environmental discourse in this country seems as fractured as conversation on issues of immigration, gun control, and abortion. Increasingly, political party affiliation is the greatest determinant for one's beliefs about climate change and attitudes about federal environmental policy. Democrats increasingly support action on climate change, and Republicans increasingly reject both the science and the policy aimed at climate change adaptation and reversal. Recently, this split has shown hopeful signs of changing course;[19] however, the consequences of decades of gridlock, denial of scientific consensus, and inaction are of profound moral, economic, social, and spiritual concern.

Environmental groups have tried a number of strategies over the last few decades to address this serious global crisis, deploying a host of scientific facts, activism efforts, and political strategies. However, research has clearly identified a significant issue for those who hope to inspire more environmentally friendly policies and practices: in the United States, the message and the messengers have not adequately accounted for political polarization.[20] Conservatives conclude that the communication around the environment has been coming from liberal sources, with liberal frameworks, promoting liberal solutions. Tribal walls go up. To act on the environment is to join the left, and for most conservatives, that is much too big of an ask.

In the last decade, however, environmental organizations have begun to recognize that a key to bipartisan action on environmental issues and climate change may lie in the language employed and the way these issues are communicated. This recognition is not just occurring in liberal-leaning environmental organizations. In a challenge to their party's dominant position, conservative environmental groups have emerged across the country, guided by leaders who aim, in their words, "to change the narrative."

I conducted research in 2018 examining the communication strategies employed by conservative environmental groups to reach members of their own party (as well as across the divide) to overcome the stark political polarization on climate change and the environment. Through researching four conservative environmental organizations and conducting semi-structured interviews with their leaders,[21] I identified three elements pertinent to our conversation on communication and polarization. Communication scholars generally ascribe great importance to these elements when examining our communication: the message, the messenger, and the audience. Building on our conversation about the power of language, this section will outline these three crucial considerations for leaders: *how* a message is communicated, *who* is doing the communicating, and the assumptions made about the *audience*.

Consider the Message

An emerging theme from my research on conservative environmental communication in the polarized United States is that the message matters. All the leaders I interviewed were clear that engaging politically conservative voters on matters of the environment is successful only when we utilize language congruent with their party's values and beliefs. For example, when talking to conservatives about solar energy, Green Tea Party activist Debbie Dooley doesn't lead with climate change or regulations on emissions. Instead, Dooley invites conservatives into a conversation around what solar power means for American energy independence, innovation, leadership, and national security.

For RepublicEn, an organization pushing for the accounting of carbon to address climate change, conversations center on the benefits of the free market, limited government, and conservative principles. Leaders of both organizations are thinking critically about the values woven through their messages; they recognize that the words they choose to talk about climate change and the environment are value laden.

One way to talk about this strategy is through the concept of "framing." Pioneered by Erving Goffman in the 1970s and developed further by Robert Entman, George Lakoff, and others, *fram-*

ing has to do with the way messages are presented through various lenses, with differing motives, every single day. Entman argues that to frame is to "select some aspects of a perceived reality and make them more salient in a communicating text, in such a way as to promote a particular problem definition, causal interpretation, moral evaluation, and/or treatment recommendation for the item described."[22] Frames are used to sell us products and to help us conceptualize different events; they serve as powerful mediators in how we see and understand the world.

For example, there have been a host of recent critiques about how media and others frame the experience of cancer patients[23] through a war metaphor. Our framing of "a war on cancer" evokes a binary of winners and losers in a violent fight. Research has highlighted that for cancer patients, language around "losing their battle with cancer" can promote unnecessary and destructive feelings of personal failure. Interestingly, framing issues using war/violence metaphors also has potential to galvanize communities, tapping into powerful moral foundations and creating the sense of urgency often required to tackle our various national issues. Framing wields incredible influence in how we understand and act on particular phenomena.

For the leaders I interviewed, offering a new narrative that embraces conservative values (the message) is core to their mission. We know that the words we use have the power to identify our politics, frame how we approach an issue, define the gravity of a problem, and limit or expand how we want others to approach a decision. Being mindful of our messages is a core component of overcoming polarization, not just on the environment, but across any issue about which people are polarized.

Consider the Messenger

A second major component in every communication event is the messenger. While the language itself can be shaped, framed, and delivered in various ways, the message is unavoidably delivered by a particular person or organization. Sometimes, it's not necessarily *what* is being said, but by *whom* that causes frustration or resistance. The messenger greatly influences how a message is perceived and understood. Often, a message's credibility depends on the perceived credibility of the messenger. For example, a male leader touting the benefits women will experience when giving birth to children may invite skepticism (and even frustration) from an audience of women. This, of course, is not necessarily because of the message, but because of the audience's perception of the lack of credibility of the messenger (who will never experience pregnancy or the birth of a child). This doesn't mean that men can't discuss pregnancy or that white individuals can't speak on racism. It means that the perceived legitimacy of messages is heavily influenced by an audience's perception of the messenger.

In my interviews, leaders of conservative environmental organizations often cited the founding of their organizations as a way to address a perceived lack of credible messengers on climate change and the environment. With the tribal realities of political polarization so stark, even the most articulate messages on the environment were still coming from messengers whose credibility conservative voters questioned—mainly a "liberal elite." One interviewee suggested that our current polarization around climate change would not be so intense had Al Gore partnered with a conservative on the Oscar-winning 2006 documentary *An Inconvenient Truth*.

Other leaders I talked with agreed that their own identities as Tea Party cofounders or free market champions are crucial in their ability to engage with their audience. Their audiences do not have much reason to question their authenticity or veracity. With a clear message rooted in conservative values and a messenger who identifies with their listeners, one final element to overcoming polarizing divisions on the environment was articulated in my interviews: a thoughtful consideration of the audience.

Consider the Audience

In traditional rhetorical studies, an audience is the group that a messenger is attempting to influence. I refer to "audience" here broadly to include anyone who is receiving a message (mediated or face-to-face). This includes those hearing from someone behind a podium, folks listening around a table of colleagues, or individuals having a one-on-one conversation.

Every communication act includes a person or persons receiving a message, and our assumptions about the people to whom our communication is directed are often greatly misguided. Such assumptions are often a direct *result* of the communication we experience in a polarized climate. However, these presumptions about others also *contribute* to our political polarization, as we make assumptions about our listeners that are based more on sound bites from their political leaders than on thoughtful conversations with one another.

For leaders of the environmental groups I studied, considering audience was of chief importance. While the dominant rhetoric of the Republican Party in the United States might depict a party resistant to environmental policy and doubtful of scientific evidence on climate change, the leaders I interviewed did not make such assumptions about Republican and other conservative voters. Citing polling, research, and personal stories, leaders of conservative environmental groups described a conservative voting base that cares deeply about environmental issues and generally recognizes the science on climate change. Unfortunately, most environmental messaging is framed in liberal-leaning values (message) and delivered by liberal-leaning organizations or elites (messenger), with the result that the content and communicator do more to spark an ideological defense than to spur productive conversation on an issue. Conservative environmental groups' observations are strongly supported by the research, which finds that attitudes around environmental issues become much less polarized when message framing and messenger are adjusted to account for the differing moral foundations and value systems of those listening.[24]

The takeaway is clear: the assumptions we make about the people we speak with shape our communication. If we assume our members, neighbors, employees, and family members operate with the same all-or-nothing approaches of political party leaders, our communication most likely becomes argumentative, negative, and misguided. Unfortunately, communicating in this way has become not only our national model, but our default communication orientation. Fortunately, there are models across the country of alternative ways of communicating with each other, to understand and find common ground.

Communicating across the Divide

Being mindful of how our language speaks to values and frames issues (message), our own credibility and identity (messenger), and the assumptions we hold about those we are speaking with (audience) prompts us to take a more critical approach to communication. This mindfulness offers opportunities to break through polarizing conflicts. As our polarization has heightened over the last few decades, a suite of tool kits, nonprofits, models, and more has emerged to suggest what a mindfulness of language might look like in practice. Leaders might explore ways to model and foster thoughtful communication in organizations, given a climate of heightened political polarization. The movement around deliberative dialogue offers one entry point for putting these ideas into practice.

The terms *dialogue* and *deliberation* both show up repeatedly in popular media, leading one to assume that they may simply be synonyms for *conversation* or even *debate*. However, dialogue and deliberation are approaches to communicating with clear goals, often challenging our ritualized communication patterns and assumptions about how to talk with one another. These approaches are important to explore. As rhetorician James A. Mackin articulates, "The quality of our communication affects the quality of our communities."[25]

Quality communication is productive, meaningful, relationship-building, and open to thoughtful and reasoned decision-making. It does not erase disagreement or division but builds connection and understanding despite our differences. Later in this chapter, I will highlight two organizations fostering these approaches and offering insight into how leaders might invite and institute mindful (quality) communication in their own organizations and communities.

Dialogue refers to communication that, at its core, seeks to understand another and build relationship. Finding a solution or lobbying is never the emphasis. This type of communication recognizes that the words we use hold the power to help us better understand another and ourselves. While our communication can build walls and foster distrust (especially when we fall back on argumentative types of communication), dialogue recognizes that our communication can build bridges and establish trust. Dialogic communication finds its roots in many persons, places, and disciplines, resulting in a diverse and thoughtful set of theories and practice.[26] Martin Buber's *I and Thou*[27] paints a picture of dialogue as a spiritual encounter between individuals, a way of being and relating to one another. Buber's work is well known among those working at interfaith dialogue and conflict resolution. Strongly philosophical in nature, it is helpful to explore what is necessary for encounter to occur.

While I won't attempt to unpack the myriad approaches to dialogue, a few dynamics of this communicative approach should be underscored.[28] Though binary in method, one helpful approach to understanding dialogue is to contrast it with a form of communication that seems to come more naturally: debate. A number of scholars and practitioners have taken this approach, comparing and contrasting these two methods of communicating.[29] The debate approach to communication is typically our go-to method, particularly in decision-making spaces.

Debate is our ritualized mode of engaging in conversation, characterized by taking sides, listening to counterarguments, and speaking to win. Communication is often predictable, as participants reiterate talking points. The aim is to convince and defend. The prevailing attitude is evaluative and critical.[30] Participants have decided there is only one possible outcome or solution—generally their own.

Dialogue is based on a different set of assumptions, orientations, and goals. As a counter to our preferred communication style, dialogue requires mindfulness and commitment since falling back on combative communication is always a temptation. Dialogue is characterized by collaboration, listening to understand, and speaking to learn. Communication pursues nuance and complexity, as the issues generally under consideration aren't black and white. The aim is to explore, elaborate, and understand. The prevailing attitude is curious and open.[31] Participants understand that there are many perspectives and that ways forward may include their own.

In many cases, dialogue is paired with deliberation, sometimes called "deliberative dialogue." Deliberation holds a similar orientation of respect for the other and a commitment to listening, while also offering opportunity to work toward a shared direction or decision. Deliberation opens up space not just for thoughtful communication to better understand one another, but for the opportunity to move forward as a group. Deliberation offers a framework to aid groups in making decisions or pursuing directions that take into account diverse voices while also recognizing the constraints that every decision brings.

On a national level, two models worth examining are the Kettering Foundation's National Issues Forums (NIF) and Essential Partners, formerly Public Conversations Project. Both groups emerged in the 1980s and '90s to facilitate and lead communication that fosters understanding within a national environment of increasing division. Each organization selects a handful of national issues to focus on every year, such as immigration or opioid abuse. Not surprisingly, both groups have selected political polarization as part of their 2019 focus.[32] Focusing on deliberative dialogue and recognition of a national environment of political polarization, NIF and Essential Partners offer three key insights for organizational leaders.

First, *these models are strategic about framing issues* in ways that "make it difficult to draw solely on ideological affiliation or ideas."[33] The language used to spark the conversation in these deliberative dialogues is intentionally transpartisan[34] in nature. Trained moderators present national issues in a language that makes it difficult for participants to fall back on their own party's go-to arguments and bumper-sticker logics. When organizations are making decisions, this attention to how an issue is introduced, framed, and presented is critical to encouraging thoughtful deliberation rather than ritualistic debate.

Second, *a trained moderator/facilitator helps guide the deliberation in an impartial and process-oriented manner.* This practice speaks to the influence of the messenger. In organizations, leaders may not always be the best candidates to guide certain decision-making processes or address conflict situations. At times inviting another member to co-lead may be key to particular processes, to ensure that the process is representative in that members see themselves in the leadership. Each of these models emphasizes impartial facilitation and a dedication to process, which includes collaboratively laying out communication agreements at the onset, ensuring that the structure supports dialogue, and discouraging debate-style communication.

Third, the *participants actually develop a deeper understanding of an issue (and each other) while gaining a sense of ownership in a chosen direction.* Many national models that practice deliberative dialogue are clear that the process is learning-centered. The more members participate and learn, the less the resistance and the greater the decision's sustainability. This participation in the process helps participants understand a decision's various trade-offs and how one approach's constraints compare with those of an alternative route.

Caveats to Constructive Communication

While mindful communication approaches open opportunities to move beyond ritualistic debate and toward shared directions and understanding, it is important to note that communication is not a silver bullet. Context is a particularly important element to consider in efforts around dialogue and deliberation. First, history demonstrates that corrupt regimes and injustice do not often yield to dialogic approaches. Attempts at dialogue are not ethical responses to most acts of violence, like the poisoning of communities or enslavement of people. Additionally, seeking mutual understanding or shared direction with persons who insist on repulsive, racist, and repugnant rhetoric (e.g., members of Westboro Baptist Church) can be unproductive at best and deeply traumatic at worst (although I wouldn't advocate for argumentation either, as that is also futile when dealing with such groups).

Second, deliberative-dialogue processes take time. I aim not to provide a prescription but to offer some frameworks and tools for communicating in a polarized context. While we often debate issues in all-or-nothing terms, the realities in our local communities are often muddy, mixed, and moving. Conflicts are often situational, our communication inherently contextual. Complexity demands time, but decisions may demand an urgency that greatly constrains efforts at deliberative dialogue.

Third, there will always be a need for debate in democratic societies. When done constructively, debate helps articulate motivations, claims, and outcomes. One of the oldest traditions in academia, debate at schools and universities across the country empowers students to speak confidently, be wary of biased sources, and produce reasoned arguments on a topic. Debate becomes unhelpful when it becomes our dominant communicative orientation, guiding our speaking and listening in all our interactions.

Conclusion

The devolution of our public discourse is sobering. Bitter, lazy, reactive, and disrespectful communication reigns supreme among leaders in various arenas of society. Our current state of polarization both reflects this communication and helps reproduce it. Leaders have an opportunity, if not an obligation, to cultivate mindful communication—counterintuitive and rarely modeled—in our organizations, civic spaces, and cultural hubs. Thinking critically about our messages, our positions as messengers, and our audience can begin to reshape the way we normally communicate. Pulling from the movements of dialogue and deliberation, leaders can model and institute communication that builds understanding and relationship, rather than cementing gridlock and distrust.

Writing for the *Integral Leadership Review*, social, peace, and environmental activist and author Tom Atlee highlights the value for leaders to examine communicative practices in models like National Issues Forums, Essential Partners, Living Room Conversations, and more. Atlee suggests:

> Integral leaders who wish to counter the incapacitating spread of polarization have . . . powerful conversational technologies to help diverse and conflicted people use their differences creatively . . . to come to useful conclusions and policies together that include and transcend their previously discordant views. Practicing and institutionalizing these conversational approaches greatly enhance our capacity to be not only collectively intelligent, but collectively wise.[35]

In chapter 1, David Brubaker highlighted a suite of social, economic, and emotional factors responsible for the polarization we see today. However, he concludes that “the rise of populism and nationalism would not have been possible without someone to give voice to the increasing marginalization and identity threat that many Americans were feeling.” With this voice leaders help call into being the world they wish to see. Our language carries power; our communication facilitates change. Let us seek the collective intelligence and wisdom the current moment demands. Let us communicate across, or in some cases in spite of, our current divide.

Notes

1. Debbie Dooley, personal interview by the author, October 31, 2018.
2. The Linguistic Society of America has lots of excellent research and resources on these distinctions. See, for example, Betty Birner, ed., "Does the Language I Speak Influence the Way I Think?," Linguistic Society of America, https://tinyurl.com/y5cnv63y.
3. Ella Tennant, "How Gendered Language Shapes the Way We See the World," Phys.org, November 29, 2017, https://tinyurl.com/y6pc56m5.
4. Lera Boroditsky, Caitlin Fausey, and Bria Long, "The Role of Language in Eye-witness Memory: Remembering Who Did It in English and Japanese," *Proceedings of the Annual Meeting of the Cognitive Science Society* 31 (2009), https://tinyurl.com/y584a47b.
5. Stephen C. Levinson, "Language and Cognition: The Cognitive Consequences of Spatial Description in Guugu Yimithirr," *Journal of Linguistic Anthropology* 7, no. 1 (1997): 98–131.
6. Birner, "Does the Language I Speak . . ."
7. Matthew Gentzkow, Jesse M. Shapiro, and Matt Taddy, "Measuring Group Differences in High-Dimensional Choices: Method and Application to Congressional Speech," National Bureau of Economic Research, March 2019, https://tinyurl .com/y6m8mcw3.
8. Teri K. Gamble and Michael Gamble, *Communication Works*, 11th ed. (New York: McGraw-Hill, 2013), 86.
9. Conor Friedersdorf, "A Better Way to Look at Most Every Political Issue," *The Atlantic*, February 11, 2018, https://tinyurl.com/y7lkqt79.
10. Friedersdorf, "A Better Way."
11. Mark Abadi, "Democrats and Republicans Speak Different Languages—and It Helps Explain Why We're So Divided," *Business Insider*, August 11, 2017, https:// tinyurl.com/y32onrao.
12. Gentzkow, Shapiro, and Taddy, "Measuring Group Differences".
13. More details on the specific algorithm Gentzkow and colleagues developed can be found in their published research, as well as here: Krysten Crawford, "American Political Speech Is Increasingly Partisan, Stanford Research Shows," *Stanford News*, July 19, 2016, https://tinyurl.com/y4a3wyal.
14. I really like Tom Syverson's reference to "second-hand discourse" as a way to capture the slogans, buzzwords, memes, GIFs, and other tools we employ to settle debates. According to Syverson, we "speak without saying much . . . we 'like' articles without actually reading them

and settle debates with retweets." His piece here is worth reading: "Linguistics Can Help Conservatives and Liberals Agree on Objective Reality Again," *Quartz*, February 23, 2017, https://tinyurl.com/h7s32uw.

15. Roman Jakobson, *Linguistics and Poetics in Style in Language* (Cambridge, MA: MIT Press, 1960), 350–77.
16. Jakobson refers to this as the "referential function" of language.
17. Jakobson refers to this as the "metalingual function" of language.
18. First posited in S. I. Hayakawa, *Language in Thought and Action* (Oxford: Harcourt, Brace, 1949).
19. At least a few polls from 2018 documented a slight uptick over recent years in belief in climate change on the part of registered Republican voters. See, for example, "Climate Concerns Increase; Most Republicans Now Acknowledge Change," Monmouth University, November 29, 2018, https://tinyurl.com/y2s3m7e5; and "Climate Change Opinions Rebound among Republican Voters," Yale Program on Climate Change Communication, May 8, 2018, https://tinyurl.com/yxfq6eyj.
20. Jesse Graham, Jonathan Haidt, and Brian A. Nosek, "Liberals and Conservatives Rely on Different Sets of Moral Foundations," *Journal of Personality and Social Psychology* 96, no. 5 (2009): 1029–46, doi:10.1037/a0015141; Aaron M. McCright and Riley E. Dunlap, "The Politicization of Climate Change and Polarization in the American Public's Views of Global Warming, 2001–2010," *The Sociological Quarterly* 52, no. 2 (2011): 155–94, doi:10.1111/j.1533-8525.2011.01198.x; Jack Zhou, "Boomerangs versus Javelins: How Polarization Constrains Communication on Climate Change," *Environmental Politics* 25, no. 5 (2016): 788–811, doi:10.1080/09644016.2016.1166602.
21. Everett N. Brubaker, "No, We're Not Kidding: Environmental Messaging by Conservatives, for Conservatives" (paper presented at Western States Communication Association Annual Conference, Seattle, WA, February 23, 2019).
22. Robert M. Entman, "Framing toward Clarification of a Fractured Paradigm," *Journal of Communication* 43, no. 4 (1993): 51–58.
23. Elena Semino, a linguist at Lancaster University in the United Kingdom, has examined the level of empowerment or disempowerment patients and family members experience in light of the use of "violence metaphors." More on Semino's work can be found here: Misha Gajewski, "May I Take Your Metaphor?—How We Talk about Cancer," *Cancer Research UK*, September 28, 2015, https://tinyurl.com/yxkpsscw.
24. Christopher Wolsko, "Expanding the Range of Environmental Values: Political Orientation, Moral Foundations, and the Common Ingroup," *Journal of Environmental Psychology* 51 (April 2017): 284–94, doi:10.1016/j.jenvp.2017.04.005.
25. Cited in Josina M. Makau and Debian L. Marty, *Dialogue & Delibera-*

tion (Long Grove, IL: Waveland Press, 2013), 1.

26. The work and writings of American social scientist Daniel Yankelovich, Russian literary theorist Mikhail Bakhtin, American quantum physicist David Bohm, German philosopher and critical social theorist Jürgen Habermas, and many others offer a rich assortment of theories and approaches to dialogue. I recommend the following for further exploration into the origins of dialogic communication: Frances Sleap, Omer Sener, and Paul Weller, *Dialogue Theories* (London: Dialogue Society, 2013) and *Dialogue Theories II* (London: Dialogue Society, 2016).

27. Martin Buber, *I and Thou* (New York: Scribner, 1958).

28. Oliver Escobar, *Public Dialogue and Deliberation: A Communication Perspective for Public Engagement Practitioners* (Edinburgh: Edinburgh Beltane, 2011), 22.

29. Escobar, *Public Dialogue and Deliberation*, 20. Citing work by Daniel Yankelovich, Stephen Littlejohn and Kathy Domenici, the Public Conversations Project, and others.

30. Deborah L. Flick, *From Debate to Dialogue: Using the Understanding Process to Transform Our Conversations* (Boulder, CO: Orchid Publications, 1998).

31. Flick, *From Debate to Dialogue.*

32. Both organizations have guides available for download: National Issues Forums, "A House Divided: What Would We Have to Give Up to Get the Political System We Want?" n.d., https://tinyurl.com/y48qy87r; Essential Partners, "Conversations across the Red-Blue Divide," October 24, 2018, https://tinyurl.com/yyeqxqpl.

33. Personal interview with Kara Dillard, Common Ground for Action Operations and Moderator Training Specialist, National Issues Forums Institute, February 11, 2019.

34. The Mediators Foundation provides a nice explanation of *transpartisan*, described as "valuing inclusive solutions that transcend and include all political party positions and promote cross-spectrum collaboration for the benefit of all." Their comparisons with bipartisanship are particularly insightful. See https://tinyurl.com/yyx5udkc.

35. Tom Atlee, "Polarization, Conversation, and Collective Intelligence," *Integral Leadership Review*, November 2018, https://tinyurl.com/o3j3w4y.

4

TRAUMA, POLARIZATION, AND CONNECTION

Carolyn E. Yoder

> They shall all sit under their own vines and under their own
> fig trees,
> and no one shall make them afraid;
> for the mouth of the Lord of hosts has spoken.
>
> —Micah 4:4

It was only nine a.m. that Monday in March 2003, but already I suspected it would be a long week. For months, the news had been full of talk about whether Iraq posed a threat to the United States. The previous day, protests against the possibility of a US-led coalition invading Iraq had erupted around the world. President George W. Bush was scheduled to address the nation that evening.

Twenty-four people from communities impacted by 9/11 had gathered for a five-day Strategies for Trauma Awareness and Resilience (STAR) training.[1] In the opening round of introductions, it was obvious the people in the room were as entrenched in their positions as was the rest of the country.

My co-facilitator and I acknowledged the high-stakes tensions worldwide and the differences in the room, then directed attention to the group guidelines and objectives for the week. We plowed through the day, trying to focus on the agenda: explaining the normal reactions of individuals and groups when trauma has shattered safety, and how this applied to their own experiences. But the division kept seeping through. To believe or not believe claims of weapons of mass destruction was a heated question. So was the morality of a preemptive war. One woman compared George W. Bush to Hitler, setting off a firestorm. One man's son had been deployed, and he feared he was heading to Iraq.

A veneer of politeness got us to Tuesday afternoon. Now the topic was the Cycles of Violence[2] that occur when trauma is not addressed (see figure 3 below): Reactions that are normal at first remain unresolved and harden into a victim identity, that is, how we were harmed becomes a dominant part of how we see ourselves. Secondary symptoms—depression, anxiety, suicide, substance abuse—set in. Individuals and groups can be stuck in a victim cycle for months, years, even generations.

Hurt people hurt people. We described how victims can cross a line and become offenders themselves, acting out their pain on others through bullying, abuse, war—all behaviors that create more victims. We identified the unreflective meaning-making narratives people adopt, often unconsciously, to keep themselves safe and seek justice: (1) us vs. them—my group over and against yours; (2) good vs. evil—seeing individuals or groups as inherently good or evil, self-identifying with good while demonizing and dehumanizing "the other"; (3) chosen trauma[3]—a group-held memory of a massive trauma at the hands of an enemy that can be reactivated to rally support if the group identity feels threatened; and (4) redemptive violence[4]—the myth that violence is necessary to protect us, that war brings peace and might makes right. We pointed out how justice is confused with revenge and how individuals and nations can carry a victim identity while also being offenders, failing to notice or acknowledge they are both.

Often a profound silence settles over the room during this part of the training as people see their trauma stories in new ways. On this day, the room was hard to read. But as the group was dispersing to find quiet spots to reflect, one of the most outspoken pro-invasion participants spoke up, a new tentativeness in his voice. "Wait, everyone," he said. "I've just realized that all of us here who support the war have closer geographic or personal ties to 9/11 than those who are against it. Do you think there's a connection?"

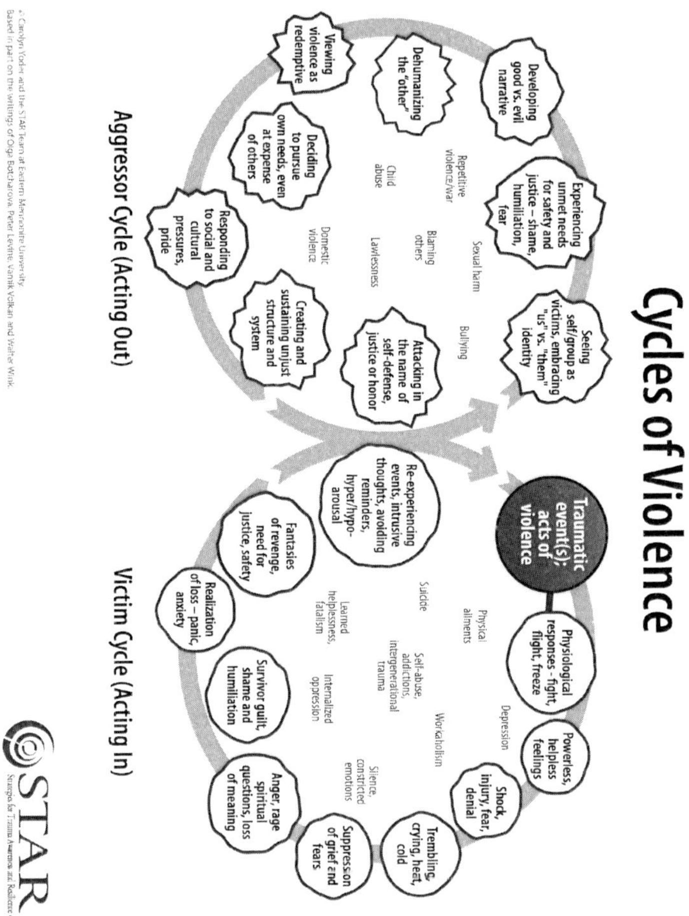

His observation marked a turning point. Positions didn't change, but the tone in the room shifted. Identifying the experience and wounds behind group members' positions had activated empathy. Supporters of the president expressed more nuance. Those against the invasion spoke with more compassion and understanding.

On the fourth day of the training, headlines of "shock and awe"[5] greeted us: the invasion had begun. The father of the deployed reservist arrived in so much back pain he had difficulty sitting and walking. He lay on a mat in the back of the room as a participant trained in massage, who was against the war, gently worked his tight muscles. Others gathered around expressing empathy and offering prayers for his son. By late morning he was able to rejoin everyone at the table.

The evaluation comments at the end of the week were thoughtful:

"I came with an us/them mentality," a supporter of the war wrote. "Now I see what I must do—face the trauma so that it doesn't come out in escalating cycles of violence."

"I leave with a feeling of humility," wrote a participant who opposed the war. "I was challenged by my feelings of tolerance/intolerance, and I grew through the process."

Trauma polarizes. Then that very polarization can be traumatic as it creates rifts and severs friendships. Scratch beneath the surface of any conflict, division, or evil, and you often find unaddressed individual and/or group trauma. The economic, social, and emotional factors David Brubaker outlines in chapter 1 as causes of polarization all can be sources of trauma.

In this chapter, I share how a trauma lens can help in understanding and addressing some aspects of division and reconnection. We'll begin with a definition of trauma and how threat and fear create a lack of safety that profoundly impacts beliefs and behaviors, fueling "othering" reactions that contribute to cycles of violence if unaddressed. We'll explore the malignancy of fanning fear and ways to prevent or break cycles of violence. We end with ways leaders can foster safety and connection.

What Is Trauma?

Trauma, from a Greek word meaning "wound," refers to an individual's or group's responses—physical, emotional, cognitive, spiritual, and relational—to traumagenic[6] events or unjust systems. *Traumagenic* means "likely to cause trauma to the people who are targeted, the perpetrators, and the witnesses." It reflects the subjective nature of how individuals and groups experience an event: what is traumatic to one may be only stressful to another. Traumagenic experiences differ from ordinary stress in intensity and/or duration and likely lead to leave survivors feeling overwhelmed and powerlessness. The belief that life is meaningful and orderly is challenged.

Traumagenic events are an inevitable part of life. Trauma can result from one-time events (natural disasters, airplane crashes) or from circumstances that are cumulative or ongoing for individuals or collectives (dignity violations, loss of a way of life, structural violence such as racism or living in poverty). Collective historical atrocities like the Holocaust, the Palestinian Nakba,[7] or the genocide of aboriginal people also are traumagenic. If unaddressed, the effects are passed on through the generations.

Safety and the Impact of Threat/Fear

My colleague Tricia[8] was driving to a consultation with an out-of-state physician when her GPS went down. Flustered, she took an east-bound exit when she needed to go west. Traffic was heavy, and she had to travel several miles before she could turn around. Suddenly she felt hot-and-cold flashes and started to cry. Her husband, Greg, tried to help by giving directions, but she screamed at him to be quiet. Panicked that they would be late, she drove faster and faster. Greg pointed out that she was driving 90 miles per hour. Her response was to yell and swear. When they finally reached their destination, a shaken Greg said plaintively, "May I please have my wife back? This woman is not my wife." Wobbly and dazed, Tricia started to laugh hysterically. She couldn't stop shaking and laughing for several minutes.

To understand how trauma impacts us, and how it relates to Tricia's experience and to polarization, we need to begin not with the psychological but with our physical body, specifically the nervous system/brain. You may be tempted to skip this section. But if you want to address fear, hate, and division using a trauma lens, you need to understand the basics of three nervous-system responses to our sense of safety or threat/fear:[9] (1) the social engagement system (face-heart); (2) mobilization (fight/flight); and (3) immobilization (freeze/collapse). Think of these as three levels of a ladder on which, without conscious thought, we move up or down according to how safe or threatened we feel.[10] The closer to the top, the greater our feeling of safety and the degree of higher, integrated brain functioning. The more we feel threat/fear, the lower we go on the ladder, the more instinct-driven and automatic our behavior becomes, and the more our higher brain function goes "offline."

1. The Social Engagement System (Face-Heart): The Highest Rung of the Ladder

Is it safe? This is the most foundational human question. Under conditions of safety and manageable everyday challenges, we navigate the world using what neuroscientist Stephen Porges calls our social engagement system.[11] Through a "face-heart" connection, we use tone of voice, facial expressions, posture, and the quality of our attention to send or receive cues of safety when interacting with others. Interpersonal neurobiologist Daniel Siegel paints a beautiful word picture of who we are when all parts of the nervous system, which includes the brain, are humming along feeling safety and trust.[12] We are:

- able to keep our body coordinated and balanced;
- attuned to how others are feeling;
- emotionally balanced;
- capable of pausing and reflecting on options before responding;
- able to modulate fear;
- insightful and self-aware;
- able to feel empathy;
- capable of morality and acting for the common good;
- in touch with our intuition and nonrational ways of knowing that fuel wisdom.

This beautiful symphony is possible because a cluster of regions in the cerebral cortex (rational brain) work together in tandem, touching and connecting the three major parts of the brain (cerebral cortex, limbic system, and brain stem,[13] receiving information from the organs and gut, and even reading signals from the brains of other people in our social world! Siegel calls this cluster "the middle prefrontal cortex."[14] For ease of reference, I'll call it "the connecting brain" throughout this chapter.

Imagine a business, a church, a mosque, a society—or a marriage—where everyone consistently functioned from this rung of the ladder. What could compel us to leave the safety, creativity, and connection to others we have in this near–garden of Eden? Threat—and fear.

2. Mobilization (Fight/Flight): The Middle of the Ladder

Our brain/nervous system is constantly scanning for danger in and around our bodies and in our social interactions with others. Porges coined the word *neuroception* to describe this surveillance system that operates far below our conscious awareness and without the rational, thinking part of our brain.[15] It differs from perception, which comes from our senses and involves a degree of awareness.

When the ground is shaking because of an earthquake, or our group is humiliated by yet another dignity violation, neuroception alerts us, and a lightning-quick assessment happens beneath our conscious awareness: Can we use our social connection and engagement skills, our first line of response, to deal with the threat? If yes, the information is routed to our rational brain, and the symphony of the connecting brain hums into action, modulating fear and engaging socially. If no, our second line of defense, mobilization with its fight/flight tornado of energy, is activated *before the rational, thinking brain is even consciously aware of the danger*. Waiting around for the slower-thinking, analyzing processes of the rational brain to figure out what to do could get us killed.

But the social engagement system with the harmonious connecting brain is now off-line to varying degrees, just as a storm knocks out power lines in parts of a city. This is what happened to Tricia. The extent of impairment and duration of the disruption depends on the intensity of the traumagenic event, the quality of social support available, and the meaning given to what happened, among other components. Fortunately, Tricia's "disconnection" was relatively brief.

3. Immobilization (Freeze/Collapse): The Lowest Rung of the Ladder

If the nervous system senses that mobilization (fight/flight) isn't enough to ensure safety, the third line of defense kicks in: immobilization. The traumagenic threat and resulting fear are so overwhelming that we become the proverbial "deer in the headlights," unable to think, move, or talk. In extreme situations, such as a brutal sexual assault, the body may go into a state of collapse. We dissociate, faint, or are so paralyzed that we look lifeless. Even though the body is immobilized, the fight/flight energy courses through our nervous system, leaving our body in a hyper-aroused state internally. Immobilization, like mobilization, happens spontaneously and is not a conscious choice.

In the twenty-first century, and in countries and communities not experiencing chronic violence, our threats are rarely the attacking-tiger type, for which mobilization/immobilization works best. More likely, our immobilization has to do with being trapped in a meeting with a verbally abusive supervisor, buckled up in a cramped airline seat when turbulence is pressing our panic button, or watching a political debate on television. We may feel immobilized by ongoing discrimination or when caught between polarized constituents. Our neuroception surveillance system recognizes threat and fear, and faithfully keeps releasing stress chemicals and hormones, fueling energy that has nowhere to go.

Trauma Aftereffects

When the fight/flight mobilization energy is used to run away or physically stave off a threat, the body can calm down afterward and return to a state of rest. But if there's no one to physically run from or fight, the surge of trauma energy is trapped in the nervous system. If not released, this undischarged, constricted energy—*not* the actual traumagenic event—is believed to be what produces many physiological trauma reactions, such as flashbacks or insomnia.[16]

Meanwhile, the below-conscious-awareness neuroception system is pressing on. Psychologist Deb Dana, a nervous-system expert, says that "because we humans are meaning-making beings, what begins as the wordless experiencing of neuroception drives the creation of a story that shapes our daily living."[17] Stories like the polarizing "us vs. them" or "good vs. evil" narratives that then affect our behavior. Meanwhile the social engagement system/connecting brain is still not fully online.

Trapped energy, neuroception-driven narratives, and a disrupted connecting brain are all normal effects of traumagenic events. We can feel shame about what we do or don't do when under the impact of fight/flight and freeze/collapse. Understanding how our automatic biological responses are fiercely devoted to keeping us safe can help us forgive ourselves. But we also need to actively address these embodied imprints of trauma. If unaddressed, they morph from normal trauma responses into cycles of violence.

Recognizing Unaddressed Trauma

Being diagnosed with post-traumatic stress disorder (PTSD)[18] isn't the only measure of whether an individual or group is traumatized. If you want to know if unaddressed trauma is affecting you, your community, or your organization, observe the *quality of the relationships* people have with themselves and each other over months, years, and centuries. If you see the acting-in and acting-out behaviors and beliefs in the Cycles of Violence diagram, there is likely an underlying current or historical trauma that has not been addressed.

Unaddressed trauma will continue to mute the symphony of the connecting brain: the ability to creatively and flexibly have empathy, extinguish fear, act according to our values, and access our intuition and inner wisdom. Individuals and groups become rigid, self-righteous, and rageful, and confuse justice and revenge. Even benign actions of others are interpreted as threats. Stephen Porges found that when we don't feel safe, we subconsciously read neutral faces as aggressive and fearful faces as angry.[19] The group of people with whom we use our heart, face, and voice to negotiate relationships and maintain safety narrows. The body remains on alert (hyperarousal) or goes numb (hypoarousal), or alternates between the two. Unaddressed trauma literally can shorten our lives[20] and is transmitted to future generations not just psychologically but through our DNA.[21]

Psychiatrist and international-conflict expert Vamik Volkan observed that societies with extensive trauma and conflict typically exhibit what John Mack has called the "egoism of victimization,"[22] a reduction in their ability to see beyond their own pain and empathize with the suffering of others. Consequently, they experience little guilt about committing retaliatory violence and fail to take responsibility for the victims and suffering created by their own actions. This dynamic can be observed whether the issue is an international conflict or something more personal, like a bitter divorce.

Addressing Trauma

Cycles of violence can be prevented, minimized, or broken by knowing how to address trauma. This means:

- releasing the physical effects of fight/flight energy to restore access to the social engagement system;
- acknowledging polarizing meaning-making narratives and exploring new stories;
- working nonviolently to transform relationships and systems to meet basic human needs for security and justice.

We will take a brief look at how each can contribute to reducing division.

Restoring the Connecting Brain

Releasing trapped energy can be as straightforward as noticing what is happening in the body after experiencing something traumagenic, and if it's safe, letting it continue Tricia's body did this spontaneously: laughter and shaking are natural ways the body releases trauma energy. So is crying and even wailing—responses we often try to shut down, fearing we're losing it. Running, brisk walking, deep breathing, or getting a massage can release trapped energy. People sometimes have the urge to kick, hit, or throw things. Safety of yourself and others always comes first.

You can release the energy behind those impulses using the Emotional Freedom Technique (EFT),[23] a simple but amazingly quick and powerful evidence-based tool where you name thoughts, feelings, and sensations while tapping acupoints (specific points where an acupuncturist would insert needles). Adults and children can learn basic EFT (even online), and it can be done individually or in groups. Activities like singing, drumming, or playing soccer with safe people can help co-regulate you (their system helps calm your system) and restore feelings of security.[24] These self-regulating and co-regulating ways of releasing trapped trauma energy will go a long way to restoring calm, clarity, and connection to others—evidence of the connecting brain.

Acknowledging Narratives

Acknowledgment, deep truth-telling to heal differences, is a way to break cycles of victimhood or violence. In the STAR approach, the acknowledgment process is guided by a set of questions applicable to individuals or to group/society narratives. (Please note caveats.[25])

STAR Acknowledgment Questions

*What was done to me/us?**

*Why me/us?** (An often-unanswerable question, so ask instead)*

*Why them? Why did they do it to me/us?***

*What did I/we do to others?**

*What did I/we fail to do?**

Sources: Fr. Michael Lapsley[26] and Olga Botcharova[27]

You'll see these questions reflected in Anna's story[28] of being sexually assaulted during her college years by a drunken classmate who forced his way into her apartment late one night. During the Supreme Court confirmation hearings for Brent Kavanaugh in 2018, Christine Blasey Ford testified that he had sexually assaulted her when they both were teenagers. As Anna listened to the proceedings about an unreported rape, feelings she had pushed down but never forgotten flooded her mind and dysregulated her body. All these years, she had carried barely suppressed anger and disgust for her assailant. Anna journaled, tapped on acupoints when she felt upset, went for long walks, talked with friends, and went to therapy. After six months, she discovered that the perpetrator lived only a few hours away and decided to confront him. (Note cautions on meeting with "the other."[29])

In a mirroring of what was happening on the national stage, the man, who like Anna was now nearly seventy, denied any knowledge of the assault. But in a departure from the national drama, he acknowledged he had had blackouts, and asked for her forgiveness if in such a state he had raped her.

Anna trusted her neuroception and perception that he was sincere and was telling the truth. She told him she needed to think about forgiving and left, pleased that she had had the courage to initiate the meeting. But once back home, fury at how unfair it was that he could go on with his life while she had to deal with the trauma overtook her, and she seethed for hours.

Suddenly, another never-forgotten but sidelined memory popped into her mind. She had begun drinking heavily after the assault. After a night of partying, she awoke with a hangover, in her own bed with but no memory of leaving the party the night before or of driving home. She had gone outside to see if her car was in the driveway. It was. Now as she remembered, Anna felt the rage drain out of her as she realized the grace she had experienced. She hadn't crashed. She hadn't gone to jail for maiming or killing someone. It didn't erase the wrongness or violation of the rape, but her heart was different. She saw herself as both victim and offender—not all good, not all bad—and in that way, no different from her offender. Gratitude for her and others' safety, and forgiveness for herself and the classmate who had raped her, washed over her without analysis, without effort, without struggle.

Anna's story illustrates the power of acknowledging a story even years later. Releasing the trauma energy that had been triggered by the hearings allowed her brain/nervous system to be in a space where she wanted to and could hear the other's story. Even though his story was not what she wanted it to be, it opened a space within to see her own failing in a way that set her free.

At that point she could have blocked the process with the oft-used defense against facing our own shadow: "I may have done x (blacked out), but I would never do y (rape someone)." But Anna stayed open to what came organically, not from her mind, but from her heart. It allowed her to forgive herself and her assailant.

This is deep truth-telling that sets us free. This is the Spirt that blows where it will. And it's our choice whether we accept or resist that divine flow.

Anna didn't consciously follow the acknowledgment questions. The following story of my own group's historical trauma[30] illustrates how the questions can be a guide to expanding a chosen trauma narrative. A group doesn't choose to be traumatized, but they may choose to view a particular event or series of events from their history as central to their identity.[31]

My family name is Yoder. Like many surnames, it comes with a group trauma history. In the Protestant Reformation of sixteenth-

and seventeenth-century Europe, Anabaptists were imprisoned, tortured, exiled, and killed by both Catholics and Protestants for their belief in the separation of church and state, refusing to serve in the military because of Jesus's command to love enemies, and practicing baptism based on an adult faith decision (*Anabaptist* was a derisive moniker meaning "re-baptizers"). When possibilities opened for immigration across the Atlantic to the New World, thousands of Anabaptist immigrants left Europe as many had already lost their citizenship and could not own land. In the United States, they encountered opportunities, but also opposition when their refusal to serve in the military and the way their tight-knit communities retained the German language resulted in harassment and hardship during most major wars. The sense of being strangers and pilgrims and not part of the mainstream continued, impacting succeeding generations.

Once embedded in a psyche, culture, or one's DNA, a chosen trauma narrative is difficult to dispel. It's not that the story is untrue or that it's wrong to remember or seek justice. The danger is the narrative's narrow focus and that the underlying trauma remains unaddressed, with grieving and mourning usually incomplete. This leaves people susceptible to othering narratives (us vs. them and good vs. evil), to redemptive violence scenarios, and to the egoism of victimization.[32]

Unlike Anna's story, which was shrouded in shame and a conspiracy of silence, "what was done to us" was easy for me to tell. I had grown up hearing it, reading it, absorbing the horror and the glory, those brave martyrs singing as they burned at the stake. My story even had a vindicating ending: The pope apologized in recent years. So did the Lutherans and the Swiss Reformed Church. In Switzerland, 2008 was proclaimed the Year of the Anabaptists.

This is hardly deep truth. Stopping with what happened to me/us can simply reinforce a sense of victimhood and smug self-righteousness. My grievance story, while true, is simply one part of my/our history. For a fuller story, I needed to use the acknowledgment questions to delve into the history of the other, as well as into Anabaptist life since the Reformation. Here are the highlights of my quest:

Why did they do it to us? In the turbulent time of the Reformation, Anabaptism looked like anarchy, upsetting the social order with the refusal to baptize babies, which was the way citizens were registered. Anabaptists were the radicals, imprisoned and killed but also impudent at times, according to transcripts of their trials and investigations.[33] A violent terrorist fringe of the Anabaptists—from which we distance ourselves, saying it was an aberration—ignited fear and wreaked havoc and death in Munster, Germany, in the mid-1500s.[34]

What we did to others: The egoism of victimization blinded us to the pain and injustice we inflicted on others as we immigrated and settled on native land. Only in recent years have we begun talking about the Doctrine of Discovery and recognizing how we benefited. During World War II, Mennonites in Germany and Ukraine collaborated with the Nazis. In Ukraine, some likely were present at a massacre of Jewish neighbors. We harmed each other too, turning the trauma energy against ourselves by splitting over and over again. In the name of being right and pure and faithful, we neglected the greatest commandment: to love one another.

What I/we failed to do: I had always identified as a member of an on-the-margins subculture, with countercultural ideas and common-good values. Encountering Drew Hart,[35] who calls himself an Anablacktivist, started me on a journey that required me to both expand and reduce my identity to include "white" in order to learn about systemic racism and privilege.

In my quest, I unearthed little I hadn't known of the Anabaptist story before. But I had never put it together in this way, and I saw myself/my group in a different light. Although it's hard to convey in words, I felt a new sense of belonging, as if I had joined the human race in a new way.

Acknowledgment can take months or even years, and it needs a degree of psychological safety. Otherwise, threat and fear interfere. It is a pivotal, integrative experience to acknowledge that we, individually or as a group, are both victims and offenders—even if our "only" offense is othering, anger, or hatred. When we learn the other's story from history books or face-to-face encounters, suspicion and hatred begin to be replaced by understanding and even compassion, a sense of affinity and humility.[36] In moving the emphasis away from who is right and who is wrong and toward recognizing our mutual stories of pain and shame, our connecting brain can come back online. Our narratives become more nuanced and can even transform from "good vs. evil" to "we are all threads in the same carpet," from "us vs. them" to "we are all connected."

Transforming Relationships and Systems

Addressing trauma doesn't end with acknowledgment. Injustice and evil may still need to be named, new alliances forged, and forgiveness sought. But the spirit in which we work on structures will be different. Releasing trauma energy and the acknowledgment questions can positively impact relationships, reduce othering, and bring a measure of safety so we can move up the ladder toward social engagement. These processes are helpful even if traumagenic events are ongoing. Activist and social worker Resmaa Menakem applies them to addressing racialized trauma, speaking specifically to "white people, black/dark people, and public safety professionals such as police." He believes that until we recognize how the trauma of race is embedded in our bodies and address it physiologically, systemic change at any depth will be difficult.[37]

Leaders: Purveyors of Trauma or Connectors of People?

Vamik Volkan, who has worked for decades with conflicted groups and societies throughout the world, describes twenty signs of large group regression that are the fallout of fear and anxiety from traumagenic events—whether natural disasters, economic factors, terrorism, or war.[38] Two of the most predictable are that (1) group members lose their individuality as they rally blindly around a central leader, and (2) the splits between good/bad and us/them intensify.[39] Those labeled "them" are often scapegoated and demonized. The role of leaders is pivotal at such junctures: they hold the potential to enflame (destructive leaders) or tame (reparative leaders). Malignant regression occurs when leaders themselves are also regressed, along with their citizens, and people are killed or lives ruined.[40] Although their actions may not be intentional or conscious, Volkan says destructive and malignant leaders escalate anxiety and fear by

- magnifying dangers;
- blurring reality and fantasy;
- barraging the public with constant reminders of vague, looming threats
- manipulating by withholding, distorting, or misrepresenting facts, goals, and situations;
- engaging in name-calling;
- labeling dissenting views unpatriotic or traitorous; and
- dehumanizing by using "us/them" and "good/evil" dichotomies.[41]

Hurt people hurt people. Destructive and malignant leaders act out their hurt. In neurobiological terms, they keep people in fight/flight or freeze/collapse mode, in a state of fear and uncertainty, searching for safety amid neuroception-driven, divisive narratives, down the ladder from their social engagement/connecting brain and a state of well-being. Reparative leaders, on the other hand, help their people to:

- separate fantasy from reality and the past from the present;
- evaluate and face realistic dangers and problem-solve;
- learn about the humanity of enemy groups/offenders;
- hold the tension of paradox;
- restore ties to families, clans, and other groups that support an individual's reconnection to reality;
- value freedom of speech and consider what is moral.[42]

Notice the overlap with Siegel's list of a well-functioning social engagement system. Reparative leaders are like an "auxiliary connecting brain," co-regulating with their presence, helping constituents find their center and live by their values, acting well in spite of threat.

Some leaders on this malignant, destructive, and reparative continuum fit somewhere in between. Perhaps *placeholders* describes leaders who perfunctorily perform duties without empathy and warmth or put out official statements that say little and miss the heart and soul of their people. This is evidence of the *hypo*arousal and freeze of trauma. When you see floundering action that is active but leads people nowhere, you are witnessing the *hyper*arousal of trauma.

At the grocery store recently, I ran into a denominational leader who served on a task force charged with finding a way forward on same-sex policy. An official report had just been released to the public. As we chatted, he steered the conversation to the polarized reaction to the report. Suddenly he started to weep, right there in the cereal aisle. Embarrassed, he turned his back to the passing shoppers and apologized for his loss of control. Then he recounted the behind-the-scenes wrestling at the meetings, the tears that had punctuated the writing of the report. I'd read the official statement—cerebral religious language as saccharine and unnourishing as Fruit Loops. It had left me feeling unconnected, disheartened. The weeping elder at the supermarket was an incarnation I could relate to.

Being a Positive Leader in Challenging Times

Leaders are as vulnerable as anyone else to the effects of trauma, whether from current, historical, or childhood traumagenic events. In fact, you may be more vulnerable because of susceptibility to secondary trauma from hearing difficult stories from constituents, being part of traumatized organizations,[43] and needing to meet the needs of others even if your community has experienced a school shooting or a hurricane and you are impacted yourself (a "shared trauma"[44]). People will look to you, for instance, amid unprecedented trauma related to climate change, for which there are no road maps. Here are three suggestions for keeping you resilient and reparative.

1. Be Aware of Your Exposure to Trauma

Many people are out of touch with the warning signals coming from their bodies that they are stressed or traumatized. One way to increase awareness of physiological stress or regulation is by using a Heart Rate Variability monitor that measures the pattern of heart rhythms to assess the degree of synchronization with the body systems. My psychotherapy clients wear this small biofeedback device during sessions, and as they talk, laugh, cry, or stop to contemplate, a light turns green (the heart rhythm is coherent and in harmony with other systems), blue (things are so-so), or red (a lack of coherence—the social engagement system/connecting brain function is diminished). Over time, clients learn the internal feeling of coherence or lack of coherence. They carry this awareness into their daily lives and can take steps to release stress in the very moment when they first notice they "feel red."

Coherence isn't about relaxation but about how to maintain calm in the midst of activity. If the light is red too often or too long, it's time to pause and take a break—maybe even an extended vacation.

2. Call Out Those Who Use Fear to Traumatize

"Don't be afraid" is the most common phrase in the Bible.[45] Sometimes those words came before a daunting assignment. They can also be words that comfort and remind us that we aren't alone.

Those who spread threat/fear send a destabilizing message. Violence-prevention researcher Joseph Bock says people of faith should challenge and confront those within their own religious traditions who preach hate or use Scripture to sanction atrocities, bigotry, and aggression.[46] It's a criminal offense to deliberately spread Ebola, polio, or measles. Is it also criminal to keep people so focused on threat and othering that they find it difficult to feel safe, dimming the ability to be reflective, modulate fear, and connect? Imagine how many preachers, pundits, and politicians would have little to say if they had to remove threat/fear from their rhetoric and social media messages.

We are wired for connection. If we don't find a way to quell the othering and fear, perhaps a traumagenic crisis like climate change will be the crack that lets the light in. When your house is burning with your children inside, you don't ask about the first responder's political affiliation, religion, race, class, sexual orientation, or gender. You just want everyone to be safe.

Our need for safety is primal and strong, but what if our wiring for connection is even stronger than our survival instincts for safety? People heroically pull others from burning cars or jump in front of approaching trains to rescue someone. Desmond Tutu, Martin Luther King Jr., and countless others didn't wait until it was safe to act. Mary Anderson and Marshall Wallace, researchers on peacebuilding, document thirteen communities around the world that developed creative strategies that kept them out of wars engulfing neighboring villages.[47] We don't know neurobiologically what loosens the grip of the fight/flight or freeze/collapse condition, allowing individuals and groups to lose the fear of death so as to act well in spite of threat.[48] We only know that their actions tell us what we're capable of at our best. How do we cultivate this ability, individually and as a society?

3. Attune to Your Heart Wisdom

Many of us associate the heart with emotions and consider the mind the place where we make our best decisions. But wisdom traditions in the sacred scriptures of many faiths recognize the heart as the center of spiritual perception, the place of knowing beyond knowing. Neuroscience meets wisdom tradition in the recognition that being in the social-engagement system/connecting brain gives us the ability to access our intuition and nonrational ways of knowing that fuel wisdom.

The saints and mystics have always known how to access this place where, in spite of current or historic trauma, we see beyond pain and receive divine guidance. Maybe that's how they were able to act well in spite of threat.

How do you access your heart wisdom? One way is to drop your attention to the center of your chest or heart area and simply listen. Leave the whirl of thoughts and emotions in your head and wait. Or intentionally take with you a single question or concern for which you want guidance.

We are in good company when we listen and know from the heart. On the ramparts of the city wall, the prophet Habakkuk, having heard from God that an invasion was coming, waited for answers.[49] The psalmist's invitation to "be still and know that I am God" (Ps 46:10) comes not from a tranquil mountaintop but from a besieged city. The world needs twenty-first-century listeners and mystics—not sequestered, but actively engaged in the splendor and messiness of the world and teaching others to listen from the heart, too.

Conclusion

Sometimes my clients find they can clarify their story by encapsulating it in a few short sentences. Here's the story of this chapter, needed now and until the day when no one will make us afraid:

We are wired for connection.
Threat/fear shatters safety and disrupts connection.
Threat/fear can be weaponized.
Unaddressed trauma fuels cycles of violence.
Addressing trauma restores connection.
Be a positive leader.
Daunting task, yes. Alone, no.
Don't be afraid.

Notes

1. STAR was developed at the Center for Justice and Peacebuilding, Eastern Mennonite University, Harrisonburg, Virginia, in 2002. It was originally funded by Church World Service for community leaders after the attacks of 9/11 in New York, Washington, and Pennsylvania. STAR now prepares leaders to address the effects of all forms of trauma in their organizations and communities.
2. Cycles of Violence © Carolyn Yoder and the STAR Team at Eastern Mennonite University. Used with permission. For downloads of this diagram and other parts of the STAR model, the Trauma Experience, and Breaking Cycles of Violence/Building Resilience, go to https://emu.edu/cjp/star/ or https://PeaceAfterTrauma.com/.
3. Vamik D. Volkan, "Transgenerational Transmissions and Chosen Traumas: An Aspect of Large-Group Identity," *SAGE Journals* 34, no. 1 (March 1, 2001), 79–97, https://tinyurl.com/y5hrkrgy.
4. Walter Wink, *The Powers That Be* (New York: Harmony, 2010), v.
5. The phrase "shock and awe" has become associated with the invasion of Iraq. Richard Sanders writes, "Developed at the Pentagon in the mid-1990s, 'shock and awe' was a doctrine designed to leave the enemy so demoralized and disoriented that its will to resist crumbled." Richard Sanders, "The Myth of 'Shock and Awe': Why the Iraqi Invasion Was a Disaster," *The Telegraph*, March 19, 2013, https://tinyurl.com/y5bdlc2h.
6. David Anderson Hooker and Amy Potter Czajkowski, "Transforming Historical Harms," Coming to the Table, Eastern Mennonite University, 2013, https://tinyurl.com/y3r5q9kn.

7. *Nakba* (literally "disaster," "catastrophe," or "cataclysm") refers to the 1948 war when more than 700,000 Palestinian Arabs—approximately half of prewar Palestine's Arab population—fled or were expelled from their homes.
8. Names have been changed. Story used with permission.
9. Deb Dana, *The Polyvagal Theory in Therapy: Engaging the Rhythm of Regulation* (New York: W. W. Norton, 2018), 7–14.
10. Deb Dana, "A Beginners Guide to Polyvagal Theory," 2018, https://tinyurl.com/y5bc8tlj.
11. Stephen W. Porges, *The Pocket Guide to the Polyvagal Theory: The Transformative Power of Feeling Safe* (New York: W. W. Norton, 2017), 26–27.
12. Daniel J. Siegel, *Pocket Guide to Interpersonal Neurobiology: An Integrative Handbook of the Mind* (New York: W. W. Norton, 2012), 27.2–3.
13. The triune brain consists of the cerebral cortex (rational, thinking brain), the limbic system (emotional and memory center and the "first-alert alarm," the amygdala), and the brain stem (instinctual brain governing automatic functions such as breathing and heart rate).
14. Siegel, *Pocket Guide to Interpersonal Neurobiology*, 27.1–3.
15. Porges, *The Pocket Guide to the Polyvagal Theory*, 19.
16. Peter A. Levine, *Waking the Tiger: Healing Trauma* (Berkeley, CA: North Atlantic Books, 1997), 19–39.
17. Dana, *The Polyvagal Theory in Therapy*, 8.
18. The DSM-5 diagnosis for post-traumatic stress disorder has eight criteria: (1) a precipitating stressor, (2) intrusive symptoms, (3) avoidance, (4) negative alterations in cognitions and mood, (5) alterations in arousal and reactivity, (6) symptoms last for more than one month, (7) symptoms are not due to medications, substances, or other illness, (8) the above significantly impact functioning. American Psychiatric Association, *Diagnostic and Statistical Manual of Mental Disorders*, vol. 5 (New York: American Psychiatric Publishing, 2013), 271–77.
19. Stephen Porges, "What Is the Polyvagal Theory?" (interview with PsychAlive.org), *YouTube*, April 23, 2018, https://tinyurl.com/yy6wnyms.
20. CDC-Kaiser Permanente, "About the CDC-Kaiser ACE Study," Centers for Disease Control and Prevention, June 14, 2016, https://tinyurl.com/y4bzvslx.
21. Olga Khazan, "Inherited Trauma Shapes Your Health," *The Atlantic*, October 16, 2018, https://tinyurl.com/yymmk5fs.
22. John E. Mack, foreword to *Cyprus: War and Adaptation: A Psychoanalytic History of Two Ethnic Groups in Conflict* by Vamik Volkan (Charlottesville: University of Virginia Press, 1979).
23. Gary Craig, "The Gary Craig Official EFT™ Training Centers," www.emofree.com or "Emotional Freedom Techniques," www.eftuniverse.com.
24. Capacitar International provides many release and self-regulation

exercises: www.capacitar.org/.

25. Caveats: The timing of when these questions are asked is critical. There are some situations for which they are inappropriate—for example, in cases of child or domestic abuse. However, survivors on a helping journey to recover from childhood trauma may find them useful in examining the choices they are making *as adults* in how they are responding. And individuals and groups who suffered unjustified attacks or structural injustice may find them useful in looking at how unaddressed trauma has trapped them in acting-in or acting-out cycles of violence.

26. Michael Lapsley, unpublished sermon preached at Cathedral of St. John the Divine in New York City, May 5, 2002.

27. Olga Botcharova, "Implementation of Track Two Diplomacy" in Forgiveness and Reconciliation, eds. Raymond G. Helmick and Rodney L. Petersen (Radnor, PA: Templeton Foundation Press, 2001), 299.

28. Name has been changed. Story used with permission.

29. It can be destabilizing for abuse survivors to meet with perpetrators or nonsupportive family members to confront abuse without preparation. Restorative justice (RJ) processes have been found to assist some survivors who request assistance in face-to-face or proxy meetings. RJ has stringent screening guidelines and an extensive preparation protocol and provides supportive accompaniment. See Judah Oudshoorn, Michelle Jackett, and Lorraine Stutzman, *The Little Book of Restorative Justice for Sexual Abuse: Hope through Trauma* (New York: Good Books, 2015).

30. I do not speak for any official Anabaptist organization or body. This is how I embodied my group's story and how I am working with it.

31. Volkan, "Transgenerational Transmissions and Chosen Traumas."

32. Anabaptists were spared falling into the redemptive-violence narrative because of our belief in nonviolence (which is often imperfectly lived out).

33. Thieleman Van Bragt, *Martyrs Mirror: The Story of Seventeen Centuries of Christian Martyrdom from the Time of Christ to A.D. 1660* (Harrisonburg, VA: Herald, 2010).

34. Shelly Pascual, "The Gruesome Story of a Radical Isis-Like Movement That Once Ruled Münster," *The Local*, May 3, 2018, https://tinyurl.com/y5rocwnm.

35. Drew G. Hart, *Trouble I've Seen: Changing the Way the Church Views Racism* (Harrisonburg, VA: Herald, 2016).

36. Botcharova, "Implementation of Track Two Diplomacy," 300.

37. Resmaa Menakem, *My Grandmother's Hands: Racialized Trauma and the Pathway to Mending Our Hearts and Bodies* (Las Vegas: Central Recovery, 2017).

38. Vamik Volkan, *Blind Trust: Large Groups and Their Leaders in Times of Crisis and Terror* (Durham, NC: Pitchstone, 2004), 60–62.

39. Volkan, *Blind Trust*, 59.
40. Volkan, *Blind Trust*, 59.
41. Vamik Volkan, quoted in Betty Booker, "*Blind Trust* Author: Leaders' Actions in Crisis Impel Conflict, Peace," *Richmond (VA) Dispatch*, October 4, 2004.
42. Booker, "*Blind Trust* Author."
43. Pat Vivian and Shana Hormann, *Organizational Trauma and Healing* (CreateSpace Independent Publishing Platform, 2013). See also the Organizational Trauma and Healing website, organizationaltraumaandhealing.com/.
44. Advisory Committee on Colleague Assistance, "Shared Trauma: Helping Clients Cope with National Events That Affect the Therapist," American Psychological Association website, accessed March 9, 2019, https://tinyurl.com/y38vjvky.
45. Richard Rohr, *Everything Belongs* (New York: Crossroads Publishing, 2003), 61.
46. Joseph G. Bock, *Sharpening Conflict Management: Religious Leadership and the Double-Edged Sword* (Westport, CT: Praeger, 2001), 97.
47. Mary B. Anderson and Marshall Wallace, *Opting Out of War: Strategies to Prevent Violent Conflict* (Boulder, CO: Lynne Rienner, 2013).
48. Botcharova, "Implementation of Track Two Diplomacy," 295–96.
49. Habakkuk 1:1–8 and 2:1.

5

WEATHERING POLARIZATION WITH RESILIENCE

Teresa J. Haase

> We have been in training for a dark time such as this, since the day we assented to come to Earth. For many decades, worldwide, souls just like us have been felled and left for dead in so many ways over and over—brought down by naiveté, by lack of love, by suddenly realizing one deadly thing or another, by not realizing something else soon enough, by being ambushed and assaulted by various cultural and personal shocks in the extreme. We have a history of being gutted, and yet remember this especially . . . we have also, of necessity, perfected the knack of resurrection. Over and over again we have been the living proof that that which has been exiled, lost, or foundered—can be restored to life again.
>
> —Dr. Clarissa Pinkola Estés

In 1944, Martha Haase, my grandmother, lived with her husband, Paul, their three boys, her parents, and her younger sister in the German province of Silesia, now part of Poland. The Soviet Red Army, assisted by Polish forces, invaded this region and forcibly expelled Silesians of German descent.[1] The Lutheran church through a broad refugee resettlement program offered the Haases safe passage to Austria. This would entail Martha traveling by train for thirty days with elderly parents and young children and leaving Paul behind to fight in the war, but they accepted the offer, knowing that staying would likely mean death. My grandfather escorted his family to the train and, not long after, was shot and killed—information Martha would not know for ten years. The journey from their home to Austria was harrowing. My father was ten, his brothers eight and four. They witnessed death, violence, desperation, and despair. Upon arrival in Austria, they were rejected by the Austrian authorities and quickly had to make different arrangements with the Lutheran church program, which sent them to Pleß, a small Bavarian village in southern Germany, where the family settled in a barn they converted to a makeshift home.

Throughout her life, Martha faced loss and hardship. She also possessed a deeply rooted determination to master life and provided for her family in any way she could. She relied on her fierce independence and domestic skills, bartering for food by sewing, and single-handedly supported her parents, younger sister, and three sons. After her older sons left home, she moved to a small apartment in the city of Karlsruhe with her youngest son and parents. Her sons went on to have successful careers in business and the military. Martha lived in her Karlsruhe apartment until 2004, when she fell, broke her hip, and went to a rehabilitation center. She died not long after her arrival there at the age of ninety-five.

Martha Haase's legacy of strength, ferocity, and persistence continues to live on in all her grandchildren. Her life story has been a continuous source of inspiration to me. Likely, the motto my father lives by—"When the going gets tough, the tough get going"—was born from his mother's life journey. It represents the power of never giving up, even in the most challenging times.

Stress and Polarization

Martha's story is testimony to one person's thriving resilience in the midst of war—political, economic, and societal polarization at its most extreme. As outlined in chapter 1, polarization is the process whereby more and more people hold opinions at opposite ends of a spectrum. The stress of polarization significantly impacts a community and its members. The current landscape of political polarization in the United States is contributing broadly to disease for at least half the population and challenging our resilience reserves. A recent report by the American Psychological Association (APA) suggests that the current political climate may be making us sick with stress.[2] For the first time in its ten-year history, the survey found a statistically significant *increase* in stress levels in the US compared to the previous year. Americans appear to be more stressed than ever, and the most commonly shared explanation is the nation's extreme political polarization. Of the more than one thousand people surveyed for the study, *57 percent* said the current political climate was a "very significant" or "somewhat significant" source of stress.

The polarization we are feeling comes from the struggle with profound differences in values and definitions of who we are as a nation. And, according to the APA study, it's not just US residents who are struggling with these issues, but Europeans as well. According to the study, people are stressed by the fast pace of change and the uncertainty of the political climate—and unpredictability is always stressful to the human brain. Living in a landscape of polarization can lead to hypervigilance, increased anxiety, a sense of loss, and a decrease in life satisfaction. It is difficult to feel resilient when polarization is at play.

Cultivating Resilience

Yet, the antidote to our anxious response to polarization is our capacity to be resilient. Resilience is the process of bouncing back from hardship or failure. In times when there is unrest and the ground is shaky, we have to rely on our internal capacity to harness our innate desire to thrive, which offers us courage, hope, assurance, and steadiness. Martha's story conveys the way she, as a single person, relied on her resilience to help her family survive. We are resilient by nature, but in times of distress we can falter and need to be reminded about how to build resilience.

Resilience is cultivated in a variety of ways. Remembering that we carry an ancestral legacy of survival and that we ourselves have come through hard times and survived is perhaps the most potent form of resilience we carry. Other ways of building resilience include cultivating stress tolerance, self-awareness, and vulnerability; embracing the unknown; and making do (ingenuity). Once we have identified how to build resilience and draw upon it, we can turn our attention to weathering the storm of polarization, which requires a process of making meaning and rebuilding.

Resilience as the Legacy of a Mighty People

Polarization often has the dizzying effect of confusing us about who we are and where we come from. It can topple even those of us who stand in a rooted legacy of compassionate values and clear identity. The first building block of resilience is remembering where we come from. The Reverend Osagyefo Uhuru Sekou, keynote speaker at the first annual 2019 MLK Service and Learning Day at Eastern Mennonite University, offered a passionate address conveying the notion that dark times are always to be expected, but that faith, hope, and a belief in community should prevail in the face of evil and despair. Rev. Sekou was invited to give the keynote because of his dedicated effort to bring Dr. Martin Luther King Jr.'s legacy to bear in real and practical ways. He reminded the audience that while Dr. King recognized that turbulent times cannot be avoided, he came from a people firmly rooted in hope for a brighter day.

> Martin Luther King comes from a tradition of a mighty people, and these mighty people had an understanding of the world that was theologically rich and dense, because they understood that . . . black people look at the darkness and they tell the truth about the darkness but they never let the darkness have the last word. And so they say interesting things, like "Jesus is a bright and morning star." And they look at the darkness and they acknowledge it, and they say, "He's a bright and a morning star." They say, "He's the lily of the valley, water in dry places." [This is] theological richness that acknowledges the darkness. It acknowledges the pain and agony and despair, and never lets it have the last word.[3]

What Sekou identifies as the strength and wisdom of a mighty people is resilience, the capacity to rise again and again in the face of adversity. We know that suffering is inevitable for human beings—as individuals and as contributors to the systems we live and work in. We cultivate resilience by taking on the wind and storms, the trials and travails of life. Individuals can grow resilience by navigating challenges, by facing with clear intention and determination the difficulties that arrive at their feet. Though we do not want to seek out encounters with destructive forces, we cannot insulate ourselves against them. When they appear, we rely on the resilience we have cultivated to get us through.

Stress Tolerance

Building resilience also begins with growing our capacity to tolerate stress. We might think that resilience arises when we are protected from difficulty—that a coddled early start in life ensures we will be prepared to endure what comes later. Research on resilience demonstrates that the opposite is true. Resilience develops because we face and overcome our difficulties. In the early 1990s, scientists created the Biosphere 2 project in Arizona as a research tool to study Earth's living systems. The project has evolved since then and allows scientists to experiment with farming and innovation in a way that doesn't harm the planet. In one of its earliest iterations, a profound discovery had to do with the wind's role in a tree's life. Scientists noticed that the trees inside Biosphere 2 grew more rapidly than they did outside the dome, but that they also fell over before reaching maturation. After studying the root systems and bark strength, they learned that the absence of wind prevented the tree from growing stress wood. Without the presence of stress wood, trees can grow quickly but cannot sustain the growth and so cannot support themselves fully. The trees were not able to buffer themselves from normal conditions. They needed the wind as a stressor to prepare them to thrive.[4]

Americans generally view stress as something to avoid. However, many faith traditions and cultures recognize that stress is a natural and expected part of life. Cultures more closely aligned with nature, weather, and seasonal cycles have created story and myth around overcoming challenge, taking cues from the natural world's capacity to rise again, grow again, and renew again.

Self-Awareness

Another important building block for growing resilience is becoming self-aware—reflecting on our strengths and shortcomings, understanding our limitations, and knowing how others experience us. Self-awareness grows from the inside. In the systems we live and work in, we look to the leaders who are setting cultural norms, affirming the values of those systems, and instituting organizational structures. As they carry out these responsibilities, they are primarily focused outside themselves. But to help a system develop resilience, leaders must also be willing to reflect on themselves, explore their internal world, and understand where their own resilience comes from. This ethos has biblical roots. In Luke 4:23, Jesus relays the teaching "Physician, heal thyself"—wisdom that has been integrated into many of the helping professions. In the counseling world, the foundation of our work rests upon the promise we make and the ethical mandate we commit to, that we will look at our own wounds and work on healing them so that we can be fully present for others without polluting the therapeutic relationship with our own suffering. When the dentist doesn't brush her own teeth and the counselor doesn't do his own healing work, patients and clients suffer. When leaders don't practice self-awareness and fail to understand where their own resilience comes from, they are ill equipped to deal with others in times of polarization, destabilization, or crisis. When they commit to self-exploration and stand firmly anchored in their own resilience, they can successfully invite others to do the same. It is this hard work, which often goes unnoticed, that yields the greatest benefits and offers the catalyst for individual and systemic triumph.

Vulnerability

Although it may seem counterintuitive, vulnerability is actually another key component of resilience. The world we live in now is asking for a different type of leader, one who can be vulnerable, who has *"a willingness to be present in the moment*; to *make hard decisions* for the long-term health of the organization; to *lead from the heart* with compassion; to *lead mindfully and with attention*; and to *be open to [their] inner center and integrity*."[5] These qualities of vulnerability are born from a capacity for self-awareness and self-reflection. Through self-awareness and a willingness to face our own suffering and challenges, understand our relational patterns, and seek feedback from others, leaders develop the capacity to be the kind of leader our world needs.

Leon Seltzer, a psychologist who works with trauma resolution, writes that it's one thing to *feel* vulnerable and quite another to let yourself *be* vulnerable. Being vulnerable suggests both a recognition and acceptance of the fact that we're *all* vulnerable, and—"paradoxically—it implies that through the very act of *being with* your vulnerability (vs. anxiously endeavoring to escape it), you can thereby transcend it, moving forward anyway with your objectives, plans, and desires."[6]

In her book *Daring Greatly*,[7] Dr. Brené Brown argues that embracing vulnerability means facing our fears and reckoning with the unpredictable nature of life. Dr. Brown has devoted twenty years to researching the paradoxical strength of vulnerability, and her work has created a paradigm shift in conceptualizing leadership and relationship in general. In his reflection of the strength of vulnerable leaders, strategy consultant Augusto Giacoman writes, "The vulnerable leader decides that she will meet that uncertainty with an open heart, willing to experience all the ups and downs that come with it. Vulnerable leaders know they can confront brutal realities head-on while maintaining faith they will ultimately prevail."[8] Through authentic relationship building and inspiring modeling, vulnerability can encourage deeper bonding, which is highly needed in times of polarization.

Safety and Security

Deeper bonding in relationships contributes to the safety and security of a system, another building block of resilience. Our basic needs as human beings have to do with feeling secure and safe. These are needs we have in our families, in our churches, and in our work. In a profound story of how vulnerability impacts the safety of an organization, NPR reporter Angus Chen outlines an experiment of sorts that took place on Shell Oil's deepwater platform Ursa. In initiating this project, employee safety was first and foremost on the mind of Rick Fox, the asset leader for Ursa, due to a rise in accidents and safety concerns. He knew that something about the way things were managed had to change. He was contacted by Clare Nuer, a leadership consultant and Holocaust survivor, who had heard about Fox's desire to change things, and offered to help. Chen writes:

> Nuer felt that management problems had a lot more to do with interior [intrapersonal] struggles than with the kinds of things typically taught in business school. Creating environments where people supported each other, she thought, would free them to make great contributions. For people to make those kinds of fundamental changes, it helped to have the involvement of not just their co-workers but their family members, too.[9]

Nuer invited Fox to come to one of her seminars, "Personal Mastery and Learning as Leadership," where Fox and his son were able to talk to each other honestly, vulnerably, and emotionally. Fox credits Nuer's seminar with repairing his relationship with his son.

Based on his personal experience, Fox invited Nuer to work with the Ursa employees. The result of Nuer's work, which required the men to talk to each other about their life histories, suffering, and related emotions, was significant and groundbreaking. By addressing the internal suffering of the men working on the oil rig and encouraging deeper connections to one another, Nuer enabled the men to change. By allowing themselves to become vulnerable, they altered "their sense of who they were and could be as men,"[10] which led to their increased comfort with one another, their sense of connection with one another, and their sense of overall personal safety, which generalized to increased safety at work.

In their study of Ursa, Robin Ely, the Diane Doerge Wilson Professor of Business Administration at Harvard Business School (HBS) and faculty chair of the HBS Gender Initiative, and Dr. Debra Meyerson, associate professor of education and (by courtesy) organizational behavior at Stanford University, note that as the men became more open about their life stories, their suffering, and their general feelings, communication in general improved. They also discovered in their fifteen years of studying oil rigs that as leaders worked to maximize the safety and well-being of coworkers and help them do their jobs effectively, the working culture for oil rig workers shifted from a "macho culture" to a culture where they "admit when they've made mistakes and explore how anxiety, stress, or lack of experience may have caused them; appreciate one another publicly; and routinely ask for and offer help."[11]

This shift in culture led to an 84 percent decline in Shell's accident rate companywide, and the company's level of productivity—in terms of numbers of barrels, efficiency, and reliability—exceeded the industry's previous benchmark.[12]

As I stated above, what initially made Rick Fox open to exploring Nuer's insight that crew members' personal struggles were affecting their performance as a team was his willingness to engage in a similar process of encounter with his son, which he describes as a transformational experience. When leaders allow themselves to be vulnerable, when they are more open and emotionally available, this leads to increased insight about building resilience among those they serve, and improves team performance.[13] Similarly, what we have come to understand through Dr. Brown's pioneering work is that vulnerability is key to successful leadership and is especially key in times of polarization when people are reeling from increased stress and need authentic relationship and community.

Embracing the Unknown

Again, though counterintuitive, vulnerability is key to facing the unknown, which is often a contributor to polarization. When the landscape shifts and suddenly the vision that once guided a system must be adapted, those of us facing the unknown may find ourselves feeling disturbed and uprooted.

Accepting Reality

One way of embracing the unknown is to accept the realities at play, which may sound paradoxical. When we encounter unknown situations, we might respond with confusion or disorientation, or our actions might emerge out of fear of the unknown. Accepting the realities in an unknown situation means accounting for facts—distinguishing between what we do know and what we need to find out. Diane Coutu, writer and former senior editor of the

Harvard Business Review, in her article "How Resilience Works," identifies a staunch acceptance of reality as one of three characteristics of resilience: "Resilient people have very sober and down-to-earth views of those parts of reality that matter for survival."[14] I think back to my grandmother, who was a very pragmatic person, albeit with sprinkles of magic and mischief. Her ability to clearly see and respond to the dangers that crossed her path allowed her to keep herself and her family safe from the horrors of war. Coutu goes on to say that "when we truly stare down reality, we prepare ourselves to act in ways that allow us to endure and survive extraordinary hardship."[15] Though much was unknown in the face of war, it seems likely my grandmother accepted the reality at hand. The family had to flee in order to survive, and she wanted to keep them together. She was raised in a farming village and had already experienced the realities of life and hard work, which helped her face the unknown with the knowledge that she was capable of doing hard things, so she trusted herself to lead the way for her family.

Accepting Ambiguity

An additional aspect of embracing the unknown has to do with accepting ambiguity. Ambiguity is a situation in which something has more than two meanings. It is a concept we stress in counselor training. When our clients are telling their story or relaying a difficult life event, we often "sit" in ambiguity. The client has their own interpretation, while the clinician may have a different interpretation. We accept both interpretations as possibilities or truths. Polarization happens as a result of dealing ineffectively with ambiguity. It is an outcome of an inability to accept that there are multiple truths or many right ways. Melanie Allen, a life coach who specializes in career development, writes that effectively dealing with ambiguity can help develop resilience, and she offers useful insight regarding the kinds of ambiguous situations leaders may encounter. Allen asserts that ambiguity emerges in situations with no familiar cues or precedents—in other words, in times when it is not possible to anticipate what will happen. On the other hand, ambiguity also shows up in complex situations in which there are a great number of cues and/or stakeholder interests to be taken into account. Too much input can throw a system off balance and create disorder and disorientation.[16]

Tolerating ambiguity takes work. It requires accepting that there are many ways to interpret the same information. It reminds us that we may need to rethink our position. It invites us to be like Columbo, Peter Falk's character in the 1960s detective show, who encountered mystery with a "not from around here" attitude. We can develop competency around managing ambiguity by learning to tolerate change, shift gears fluidly, decide and act without having the total picture, tolerate situations where things are up in the air, and tolerate risk and uncertainty. In his article "Dealing with Ambiguity: The New Business Imperative," Colin Shaw, founder and CEO of Beyond Philosophy, an organization devoted to customer service, shares ten tips for dealing with ambiguity. Though intended specifically for leaders, they are helpful to all of us. His most salient tips are these: listen to your voice—your gut, listen to advice from trusted colleagues and from colleagues who have differing opinions, and be confident in yourself and in your abilities.[17] Effectively managing ambiguity, especially when paired with an acceptance of the realities at play, can cultivate a deeper comfort in uncertain times.

Ingenuity

Coutu also identified ingenuity—"making do with whatever is at hand"[18]—as a key to building resilience. In the case of my grandmother, her family's survival was dependent upon her sewing skills. She sewed for bakers to barter for bread, for farmers to barter for cheese and produce, for soldiers for whatever money they could afford. She made do with what she had and got creative. She got crafty and made clothes for her children from bags. She also pulled from her ancestral and local knowledge of plants and medicinal herbs to treat wounds and illnesses. Though her children felt isolated and othered because they were considered "refugees" and "different," given that they were a Lutheran family living in a staunchly Catholic community, they never went without having their basic needs met. And to offset the otherness they felt, my grandmother supplied them with a quick wit, encouraged intellect and athleticism, and promoted a strong work ethic, all of which helped them succeed in life.

Leaders in turbulent times can act similarly, first by looking inward and recognizing their own strengths, the realities at hand, and ways in which they can address needs and gaps with ingenuity and improvisation. Leading through turbulent times begins with an inward reckoning, with acceptance that resilience is innate, "a way of facing and understanding the world that is deeply etched into a person's mind and soul."[19]

Making Meaning

Once we have an understanding of what contributes to building resilience and how to draw from our own resilience, we can begin to make meaning of the turbulence around us. We are anchored in and aware of our own strength. Making meaning is an active process whereby we construct a narrative around what is happening or has happened. We do this in everyday life, and it is especially helpful to make meaning in times of crisis, stress, or distress and when facing the death or loss of a loved one. The capacity to make meaning is what makes us human. Holocaust survivors Elie Wiesel and Viktor Frankl are exemplary models for making meaning from intense, horrifying, and polarizing times. Their explorations on suffering and how to find meaning in it have guided countless people navigating times of distress and crisis. Most relevant to this discussion is Frankl's assertion in *Man's Search for Meaning* that "everything can be taken from a man but one thing: the last of the human freedoms—to choose one's attitude in any given set of circumstances, to choose one's own way."[20] Here, as Frankl reflects back and makes meaning of his experience as a concentration camp survivor, he describes the source of his resilience as his power to choose his response. Freedom of choice when it comes to viewing a situation, responding to a situation, and thinking about a situation contributes to how well we can weather turbulent times. When we choose to view a difficult situation as only negative, we foreclose on the possibility of drawing meaning from it. When we choose to view a difficult situation, a disagreement, or a differing opinion in the context of fear, we shut out the humanity of the other person. As stated earlier, making meaning is what makes us human, and polarization at its worst creates an environment where it is easy for people to dehumanize one another and where fear is the driving force. Dr. Brené Brown, in an interview with Krista Tippett on the public radio program *On Being*, discusses her research on belonging and notes:

> We are the most dangerous to ourselves and to each other, and even to the people we love, when we're in fear. And so when you have a situation where you've got—you're in a small town; you're either an ethnic minority, you're a progressive, or—whoever you are . . . here's the thing that I thought was so important: that while the inextricable connection between human beings cannot be severed, it can be forgotten. And we need moments of collective joy, and we need moments and experiences of collective pain. We need to find ways to come together in those moments.[21]

I would add that we need to make collective meaning from these moments of joy or pain or difference or tension. When we co-construct meaning, we remember that we are greater than our strife—we are connected by the Spirit, by the divine, by the light, and ultimately by love. When we choose to view a difficult situation as an opportunity for growth, we allow space for meaning to be cultivated. This effectively undermines the power of polarization and taps into our innate drive to thrive—our resilience.

Weathering the Storm

Each of the aforementioned building blocks of resilience is vital. Facing reality without making meaning of hardship creates a vortex—a void—and leaves the people in a system with the feeling of being on an unanchored ship, listing and drifting out to stormy seas. When we encounter difficulty and just move on from it without making meaning, we lose the opportunity to grow from the difficulty. If Viktor Frankl had not made meaning of his experience, he would not have had the capacity to write his story, and we would not, to this day, be gleaning from his wisdom.

The need to control and account for all things without embracing the unknown prevents beautiful and creative possibilities from being birthed. Polarity thrives on a culture of black-and-white thinking. Leaving room for the gray, for the emergent, for the wind to do its work fosters resilience.

In her letter to a young activist, Dr. Clarissa Pinkola Estés—an internationally recognized scholar, award-winning poet, Diplomate Senior Jungian psychoanalyst, and cantadora (keeper of the old stories in the Latina tradition)—offers this profound guidance for facing turbulent times in her "Letter "To a Young Activist during Troubled Times":

> One of the most calming and powerful actions you can do to intervene in a stormy world is to stand up and show your soul. . . . The light of the soul throws sparks, can send up flares, builds signal fires, causes proper matters to catch fire. To display the lantern of soul in shadowy times like these—to be fierce and to show mercy toward others; both are acts of immense bravery and greatest necessity. *Struggling souls catch light from other souls who are fully lit and willing to show it. If you would help to calm the tumult, this is one of the strongest things you can do.*[22]

I understand "showing your soul" to mean drawing upon resilience—the self-awareness, vulnerability, willingness to face uncertainty and embrace ambiguity, and capacity to make do with whatever you have and make meaning of the experience. Being fierce and merciful at once is a beautiful way to manifest resilience and is vital in turbulent times. Estés also reminds us in her letter that we have been through dark times before and have survived, just as the ancestors did. Sekou pleaded for us to remember in times of turbulence and polarization that those who came before us and traversed harrowing times found a way to rebuild again. They leave us with a legacy of resilience.

Self-Care

Weathering the storm, especially if we are leaders, requires us to take good care of ourselves. This can be difficult in times of distress when those we serve need support and leadership. The important adage about putting the oxygen mask on ourselves if we want to be of any use to those who are more vulnerable than we are is an expression of a broader principle—we must heal ourselves before we can begin to do the work of healing others or the systems we work in—and important to keep in mind. Self-care is often touted, but rarely practiced, especially in professions that rely on human interaction and interpersonal support. Yet self-care mitigates the stress that many of us feel as we navigate these polarizing times.

Simple ways to practice self-care include taking time for reflection, prayer, or meditation in silence and/or in nature. Walking in the woods or on a quiet path can still the mind and calm the heart. Time with loved ones, including pets, can also be immensely gratifying. Listening to or playing music—doing any activity that brings joy—can be rejuvenating and renewing. And finally, practicing gratitude, especially for those who support us—those who share their personal gifts to keep the ship sailing—is a good way to remember that we are not alone in our work. This inevitably helps us feel more resilient and able to tackle the difficulties ahead.

Maintaining Resilience

Self-care is an important way to replenish our reserves of the resilience we have cultivated. Simple examples include taking a day off to recover from illness, scheduling meetings to accommodate working parents, encouraging a work-life balance, and taking time for periods of rest or stillness. As addressed earlier, more of us are stressed than not, which means our resilience tanks are low. We need guidance and direction about how to fuel back up, and we need leaders who can show us the way. As Sekou says, as Estés writes, and as my grandmother demonstrated, dark times will come, but we are meant to rebuild, re-create, rebound, and rise up.

In sum, we build resilience by embracing our humanity. This does not mean that fear isn't present or that doubt isn't present, but that we heed Frankl's wisdom and remember that we have the freedom to choose how we respond in times of turbulence. Polarization capitalizes on fear and on black-and-white thinking, and it undermines our humanity. It confuses and disorients us, so we forget who we are and where we come from. Polarization creates anxiety and increases stress. To counter its destructive impact, we must draw upon and cultivate our innate capacity for resilience. In times that divide and challenge us, it is imperative to remember that we are resilient creatures by nature and therefore are equipped active in cultivating resilience in ourselves and in those we serve.

Notes

1. *Encyclopaedia Britannica Online*, s.v. "Silesia," https://tinyurl.com/yyx-ufhku.
2. Melanie Greenberg, "Americans Just Broke a New Record for Stress and Anxiety," *Psychology Today*, February 19, 2017, https://tinyurl.com/y35f32f6.
3. Osagyefo Uhuru Sekou, keynote address for the Rev. Dr. Martin Luther King Jr. Service and Learning Day, Eastern Mennonite University, Harrisonburg, VA, January 21, 2019.
4. Travis Brownley, "The Necessity of Stress," *Heads and Tales at Marin Academy*, December 12, 2013, https://tinyurl.com/pzpxllo.
5. Robert Mulhall, "Leading with Vulnerability: How Being Vulnerable Can Serve—Not Harm—You as a Leader," The Crossland Group, https://tinyurl.com/y6j56p7d; emphasis in original.
6. Leon Seltzer, "How Vulnerable Should You Let Yourself Be?," *Psychology Today*, January 3, 2018, https://tinyurl.com/y4y8xf8d.
7. Brené Brown, *Daring Greatly: How the Courage to Be Vulnerable Transforms the Way We Live, Love, Parent, and Lead* (London: Penguin Books, 2016).
8. Augusto Giacoman, "The Strength of Vulnerable Leaders," Strategy Business, November 29, 2017, https://tinyurl.com/yyyrrkhk.
9. Angus Chen, "Invisibilia: How Learning to Be Vulnerable Can Make Life Safer," *NPR*, June 17, 2016, https://tinyurl.com/y773wfkf.
10. Chen, "Invisibilia."
11. Robin J. Ely and Debra Meyerson, "Unmasking Manly Men," *Harvard Business Review*, July–August 2008, https://tinyurl.com/yy6z7ml6.
12. Ely and Meyerson, "Unmasking Manly Men."

13. Giacoman, "The Strength of Vulnerable Leaders."
14. Diane Coutu, "How Resilience Works," *Harvard Business Review,* May 2002, https://tinyurl.com/pcpsk8o.
15. Coutu, "How Resilience Works."
16. Melanie Allen, "Dealing with Ambiguity and Developing Resilience," Melanie Allen Life Coaching and Career Development, https://tinyurl.com/y5osvr7n.
17. Colin Shaw, "Dealing with Ambiguity: The New Business Imperative," *Beyond Philosophy Blog*, September 9, 2013, https://tinyurl.com/y43jyk4u.
18. Coutu, "How Resilience Works."
19. Coutu, "How Resilience Works."
20. Viktor Frankl, *Man's Search for Meaning* (Boston: Beacon Press, 2006), 86.
21. Brené Brown, "Strong Back, Soft Front, Wild Heart," *On Being*, February 8, 2018, https://tinyurl.com/ycn7qmwt.
22. Clarissa Pinkola Estés, "Letter to a Young Activist during Troubled Times," Maven Productions, https://tinyurl.com/y64w7ayl; emphasis added.

6

TRANSFORMING POLARIZATION

David R. Brubaker

> Never treat others with contempt, even if you believe they deserve it. First, your contempt makes any persuasion of others impossible, because no one has ever been insulted into agreement. Second, you may be wrong to assume that certain people are beyond reason.
>
> —Arthur C. Brooks

The "Tent of Nations" was established in 2001–2002 by the Nassar family, one of the few Palestinian Christian families still farming in the fertile hill country near Bethlehem in the West Bank. The 100-acre Nassar family farm and orchard is ringed by Israeli settlements and the Separation Wall, with no access to running water or electricity.[1]

The Tent of Nations seeks to build bridges between people, and between people and the land. It has become an international peace center attracting thousands of people annually. International visitors join together to plant trees, harvest olives and fruit, teach at the Women's Education Center, lead activities in Summer Children's Camp, and work together in pursuit of a just peace through nonviolent action.[2]

Daoud Nassar, Director of the Tent of Nations, identifies the four principles of the organization, and thus of his family, as follows:

1. We refuse to be victims.
2. We refuse to hate.
3. We act based on our faith.
4. We believe that justice will in the end prevail.

For Daoud and his family, the core motto is simply "We refuse to be enemies." Daoud says that "our job is to open people up" and to do so by acting differently from what others expect. "When you act in a different way, in a way the other does not expect, you are in charge."

According to Middle East Studies scholar Timothy Seidel, Tent of Nations is simultaneously a "locus of resistance" and a "center for transnational solidarity." Deeply committed to nonviolent methods of resistance, the Nassar family has fought in Israeli courts for over twenty years to protect their ownership of the land. As Daher Nassar, Daoud's brother, told Seidel, "When you still plant olive trees, you hope that one day it will change. I have hope."[3]

In addition to its steadfast resistance in holding on to its land, the Nassar family invites visitors from around the world to live and work with them. Seidel terms these efforts "counter-mapping practices," as they are deliberately designed to challenge the assumption that only one identity group can occupy this land.

The Nassar family is thus engaging in two refusals—first, a refusal to abandon their ancestral land; second, a refusal to be enemies with those who are pressuring them to do so. At the same time, they are practicing two invitations—first, an invitation to friends from around the world to join them and work with them; second, an invitation to their Israeli neighbors to live as friends rather than enemies.

This combination—refusing injustice and enmity while welcoming friendship and solidarity—requires great strength and faith in something larger than ourselves. The Nassar family persists through harassment, threats, and destruction of their olive trees. Their commitment to live as loving neighbors in one of the world's most highly polarized contexts provides a model of what is possible for all of us who live in polarized societies.

Polarization operates at multiple levels—inside of us (intrapersonal), between us as individuals (interpersonal), among us as an organization or a congregation, and within our communities, nations, and world. In order to successfully transform polarization, therefore, we must develop strategies to address it at each of these levels. This chapter focuses on transforming polarization, starting at the most fundamental level—the intrapersonal.

Intrapersonal Transformation

Overcoming polarization begins with an individual commitment to think and act in new ways. In the face of profound differences and perceived threat, the natural human response is to flee, fight, or freeze. Each of these choices may be appropriate in some situations, but they are far from transformational. I should know . . . I've practiced all of them.

> At the weekly lunch meeting of a community service club, a member at my table comments disparagingly about the "socialist candidates" of a particular political party and the "idiots" who would support them. Since I do not know the member and his comment was not addressed to me, I decide to ignore the demeaning quip. The following week, I note where the critical member was sitting and quietly slip to another table.

> A respected friend posts frequently on Facebook about issues such as criminal justice that have become highly politicized. He has several extremely critical friends (whom he refuses on principle to unfriend) who consistently berate him for his views. Upset by these personal attacks, I finally decide to (virtually) come to my friend's defense. I praise my friend's character, support his logic, and angrily reprimand his critics. It seems to work for a week or two, until the disparaging comments again proliferate.

> We are gathering for a meeting and chatting about the news when a participant comments loudly that "anyone who supports this president is a racist and sexist bigot!" I immediately think, "Some of those supporters are my family members and friends, and you have no right to paint them all with one brush!" But I freeze, as does every other person in the room. Our choice to stay quiet is not conscious but more of an instinct. The very next comment comes from the chairperson, who says simply, "I think it's time to begin the meeting."

While my responses in these situations were defensible, none of them was effective. Fleeing from a boorish club member only ensures that other members will likely endure his demeaning comments. Fighting back, even in defense of a friend, yields at best a temporary victory. And freezing in response to a generalized accusation only reinforces the speaker's prejudices. If I wish to transform polarization, I must begin by transforming my thoughts and actions. Here are three ways to do so.

1. Refuse contempt.

> Arthur Brooks, president of the American Enterprise Institute, correctly observes that "we are living in a culture of contempt." Brooks defines *contempt* as "anger mixed with disgust" and suggests that if we want to solve the polarization problem, we will have to address the contempt problem. Civility and tolerance are insufficient tools to confront contempt, Brooks argues. Rather, Brooks cites the teachings of the Dalai Lama and urges "kindness and warm-heartedness [as] the anti-venom for the poisonous contempt coursing through the veins of our political discourse."[4]

2. Honor dignity.

> As mentioned in chapter 2, Donna Hicks writes powerfully about the imperative to honor the dignity of every human being. Hicks distinguishes between "respect," which must be earned, and "dignity," which is an inherent property of all humans. Thus, "although everyone has dignity, not everyone deserves respect."[5] A commitment to honor dignity tends to elicit the noblest behavior from others, as "what makes you violent is the perception that you are being held in contempt."[6]

3. Broaden binaries.

> Polarization is the result of binary thinking taken to its logical extreme. As Everett Brubaker discussed in chapter 3, the nature of the English language tempts us to frame complex realities as simple binaries. Pollsters ask respondents if they either "support" or "do not support" a particular candidate, ignoring the reality that a typical voter will likely support some aspects of a candidate's platform and not others. Broadening beyond binary thinking is first and foremost an individual choice. Despite the limitations of our language and our political discourse, are we able to extend beyond "either/or" to encompass not only "both/and" but also multiple additional options?

If I commit to refuse contempt, to honor dignity, and to broaden binaries, my interactions with others will begin to transform. If someone I'm in conversation with senses that I consider them to be "beneath contempt," their behavior is much more likely to become contemptable. Likewise, if my conversation partner senses that my overarching commitment is to honor their inherent dignity, they are more inclined to behave in dignified ways. And if I decline to frame every debate in binary terms ("Are you for it or against it?"), I'm likely to discover additional options in the course of a conversation. Transforming polarization must start with transforming oneself.

Interpersonal Transformation

We experience polarization primarily in the context of our interpersonal relationships. We may encounter it at the extended-family holiday gathering, where an opinionated uncle launches into his annual tirade. More painfully, polarization may emerge among close friends or between spouses and partners. Today, polarizing dynamics are more likely to explode on social media than they are in a face-to-face conversation, given the distancing effect of technology. No matter what the arena, the cause of the polarization dynamic may be unrelated to politics, as human beings are capable of polarizing over virtually any disagreement.

The following commitments contribute to overcoming interpersonal polarization.

1. Seek first to understand, then to be understood (St. Francis).

> There is no more important guidance than that offered by St. Francis some nine centuries ago. The most useful prompt for depolarizing a conversation may be simply "Help me understand your perspective." When asked with genuine intent, it signals both an *interest* in understanding the other's perspective and a genuine *regard* for the experiences that might have led the person to adopt such a viewpoint. Paraphrasing or summarizing the other's perspective increases the likelihood that they will notice the effort to understand their viewpoint.

2. Invite disagreement.

> While clearly stating one's own beliefs is important, so is the willingness to invite the other person to disagree. I regularly encourage students in my university courses to "please disagree with the instructor." First, disagreement makes class discussions much more interesting. Second, I learn more from those who disagree with me than from

> those who agree. If I want to both grow in my own understanding and contribute to depolarizing my relationships, I will make it safe for others to disagree with me.

3. Stay connected.

> Perhaps the most troubling trait of polarization is that it compels us to cut off relationships with those with whom we disagree. Granted, there are times when ending a relationship is the most responsible course, such as when a relationship has become emotionally, sexually, or physically abusive. But staying connected with those with whom we disagree keeps the conversation going and increases the likelihood that we will eventually reach greater understanding.

If I can seek first to understand, to invite disagreement, and to stay connected, the likelihood of losing relationships due to polarization shrinks dramatically. I may still unfriend some acquaintances on Facebook due to their shrill political posts or personal attacks, but genuine friends and family members tend to stay connected when there is a commitment to understanding and dignity. I have yet to lose a relationship with someone I cared about but with whom I profoundly disagreed, when I have committed to these three principles.

Congregational Transformation

We also experience polarization in the communities and organizations of which we are part. As summarized in the introduction, several decades before our current political impasses former Alban Institute consultant Speed Leas identified conflict escalation dynamics that produce polarization in congregations. Seldom does a particular issue cause polarization; rather, the history, attitude, and processes we bring to our engagement with an issue feed the dynamic. This composite account from several congregations with which I've consulted illustrates how conflict can quickly escalate to the point of polarizing a congregation.

> The Placid Hills congregation is located in a suburban community on the edge of a large metropolitan area in the southeastern United States. It was founded in the early 1960s as part of the post-war boom in both housing developments and congregational formation, and is affiliated with a major Protestant denomination. The founding minister, a beloved father figure

for many in the congregation, remained in leadership for nearly thirty years before retiring in the same community in 1990.

Succeeding ministers experienced much shorter tenures, with none remaining more than six or seven years. The current lead minister, Rev. Sally Smith, came to the Placid Hills congregation five years ago after a successful ten-year tenure at another congregation. Rev. Smith was recently asked by a same-sex couple in the congregation to perform their wedding ceremony in the sanctuary. She replied that she would be honored to do so but would want to talk with the congregational council before confirming her decision. The council narrowly affirmed her right to do so.

As news of the planned ceremony rippled through the congregation, some congregants expressed support for Rev. Smith's decision and others voiced deep concern. Although the denomination with which Placid Hills is affiliated had previously granted ministers the freedom to perform same-sex ceremonies, many congregations in this conservative part of the country were hesitant to do so. The membership of Placid Hills reflected the divisions within the community, with about a third of the membership supporting same-sex marriage, a third opposed, and a third not expressing a strong opinion.[7]

Last week Rev. Smith learned that a petition was circulating among members at Placid Hills calling for her to either refuse to perform the ceremony or to resign. Rev. Smith was particularly hurt to discover that one of her associate ministers, Rev. Jeff Jones, was actively promoting the petition effort while declining to sign it himself.

As news of the petition drive tore through the congregation, a second group organized to support Rev. Smith and her willingness to perform the wedding ceremony. Several leading lay members invited others to join them in writing "letters of support" for Rev. Smith to members of the congregational council. The suggested text for the letters included a clear demand that the petitioners be publicly rebuked by the council.

Within weeks, the conflict had escalated from Level Two (a disagreement) to Level Four (fight-flight), with both groups convinced that the only realistic outcome would be for the other group to leave the congregation. Rev. Smith and Rev. Jones were also barely speaking with each other, each convinced that the other was leading the charge to tear apart the congregation. Placid Hills had polarized.

How might we understand this composite story of a polarizing congregation? First, the identified issue is almost never the real (underlying) issue. Placid Hills had also experienced a wrenching conflict in the 1970s over the calling of its first female associate minister. While the founding minister expended considerable relational capital to bring a woman associate on board, several families left the congregation over their opposition to this change. This history suggests that the underlying issues relate to questions of theological interpretation, power, and authority, rather than to the specific questions of ordination of women or same-sex marriage.

Second, the identified issue revealed, rather than caused, the rifts that were present in the congregation and between its ordained leaders. When conflict quickly escalates over any issue, it is telling us that the divisions were already deeply embedded in the congregational system. The instinct among some members to immediately draft a petition against Rev. Smith's leadership revealed that their opposition to her leadership was already well established. It only took a spark to get a fire going. Likewise, the relationship between Rev. Jones and Rev. Smith had been deteriorating for several years.

Finally, the pattern of a series of relatively short ministerial tenures after the retirement of a beloved, long-term founding minister reveals that the opposition to Rev. Smith is occurring "on schedule"—about five years into a new pastorate. Congregations that do not properly grieve the loss of a beloved senior minister inevitably find that they resist forming long-term relationships with any successor. Having never let go of their founding minister, Placid Hills now instinctively rejects every one of his successors after a brief (but always hopeful) honeymoon period.

Congregational leaders who desire to dismantle polarizing dynamics are advised to incarnate the following principles:

1. Unearth the underlying issues rather than debate the identified issue.

> The identified issue inevitably attracts obsessive attention, with attendant efforts to structure dialogue sessions and schedule educational events. While such efforts have their place, one unintended consequence is to problematize and marginalize the individual or group on whom the identified issue has focused. If we dig deeper, we often find that issues of power, authority, and decision-making (along with who has the right to exercise all three) are at the root of the conflict. These underlying issues concern all members of the congregation, not just the few members on which we have overfocused.

2. Remember that as goes the leadership, so goes the congregation.

> This maxim, first introduced in chapter 2, applies both to the ordained clergy and to key lay leaders, as together they define the "leadership" of any congregation. The most important variable in determining whether a congregation "splits" has little to do with the identified issue and almost everything to do with the leadership. If the leadership (clergy and lay) stays together, despite genuine disagreements, the congregation invariably does as well. If the leadership splinters, the congregation normally does likewise.

3. Examine historical patterns.

> As demonstrated by the Placid Hills composite case, a pattern of short-term ministerial tenures and conflicted endings suggests unresolved trauma and unproductive attitudes toward disagreement and conflict. One of the best ways to uncover these historic patterns is through a "history-boarding process," whereby a congregation collectively recalls and analyzes its own history through a facilitated exercise.[8] Once the patterns are identified, the congregation gains the ability to renegotiate its future with a different set of assumptions and commitments.

Congregations can break out of polarizing patterns. Doing so requires a commitment from leaders to unearth the underlying issues, stay together as a group, and name the patterns that are driving congregational behavior. Congregations that are proactive in these areas do not polarize.

Community and Society

After proposing ten possible causes of polarization in chapter 1, I identified three approaches to reducing polarization in our communities and society. I revisit that list below, concluding with what I believe will be the most productive strategy—rebuilding civil society.

1. Change the Political Culture and Structure

Multiple authors, including political scientists Thomas Mann and Norman Ornstein,[9] have proposed a variety of options to fix our polarized political culture and structure. These reforms range from nonpartisan redistricting to ranked-choice voting[10] to reducing the influence of money in politics. Each of these ideas, if implemented, would contribute to a democratic system that more fairly represents the average voter.

Katherine Gehl and Michael Porter of the Centrist Project advocate such reforms while proposing that the overarching problem in our political culture and structure is the "political duopoly" enjoyed by the Republican and Democratic parties.[11] To introduce genuine competition into our two-party system would require significantly restructuring the election process, something that will inspire bipartisan opposition from the two major parties that now control our binary political system.

Our political structure and culture desperately need to be reformed to become more representative of all citizens and less captivated by the two dominant parties. Mann and Ornstein, Gehl and Porter, and others have provided the road map for such a reformation. However, it will likely require an even more profound crisis than our current level of polarization to provoke such changes.

2. Change the Social/Religious Culture

Multiple faith-based authors, including Presbyterian professor James Calvin Davis, urge greater civility, unity, and moral leadership.[12] Davis urges his readers to practice the "virtues of civility," including patience, humility, integrity, and mutual respect. Writing explicitly for those in the Christian tradition, Davis also urges unity within the church. "The church's faithfulness is not threatened by theological error as much as it is by the division that results from our disagreements."[13]

David Gushee and Colin Holtz, in *Moral Leadership for a Divided Age*,[14] profile fourteen people "who dared to change our world." The leaders they examine are women and men from multiple religious traditions and countries, ranging from William Wilberforce to Malala Yousafzai. According to Gushee and Holtz, all fourteen shared a commitment to transparency and humility and to enlarging their "circle of moral concern"—a demonstration of compassion for all of humanity—not just for those who looked and believed as they did.

These faith-based authors offer a stirring vision of what true moral leadership and united religious communities would look like. However, the political homogenization of religious communities over the last forty years has mirrored the "sorting" that is taking place throughout our geographic communities. As the *Baptist News* quipped, Sunday morning is "becoming the most politically segregated hour in America."[15] If religious communities are truly to save us from our polarized paralysis, many will first have to reform themselves.

3. Rebuild Civil Society

Many authors, including Yuval Levin, the editor of *National Affairs*, advocate for rebuilding the "mediating institutions" that occupy the middle ground between the individual and the state—communities, congregations, and civil society.[16] Levin views these traditional institutions as "counter cultural agents of resistance" that offer alternatives to the domination of politics and the state. Levin proposes a political application of the Roman Catholic principle of subsidiarity—"putting power, authority, and significance as close to the level of the interpersonal community as reasonably possible."[17]

In short, one solution to societal polarization may be localism—cooperative efforts to improve our local communities. As we saw in chapter 2 in the Faith in Action story, the truly creative initiatives that are overcoming polarization are happening not at the national level but at the local one. When we focus less on Washington and more on our own communities and congregations, we discover myriad opportunities for overcoming the polarizing divisions that surround us. I believe that the most significant opportunity lies within our religious communities.

Religion and Polarization

While congregations can themselves become polarized, healthy congregations are an essential ingredient of healthy communities. In 2000 the Harvard political scientist Robert Putnam released *Bowling Alone*, a prodigiously researched and influential book on the decline of "social capital" in the United States. According to Putnam, *social capital* refers to "connections among individuals—social networks and the norms of reciprocity and trustworthiness that arise from them."[18] Putnam documented the declining participation in voluntary associations of all kinds—civic associations, PTAs, congregations, neighborhood groups, and even bowling leagues (thus the title of the book). He noted that such connections are essential to a healthy democratic society and warned of the consequences for our society if the decline continued.

In *Bowling Alone*, Putnam observed that religious congregations are the "primary repository of social capital in America," as they gather more people on a weekly basis than any other voluntary association.[19] This insight prompted Putnam and a colleague from Notre Dame University to write *American Grace: How Religion Divides and Unites Us* in 2010. Despite the subtitle, they focus more on religion's role in uniting than in dividing us. As the authors note in the first chapter, "America peacefully combines a high degree of religious devotion with tremendous religious diversity."[20]

Such "religious devotion" has slipped dramatically in the last three decades. Those who consider themselves to be "nones" (who claim no religious affiliation) are now as numerous as those who profess to be evangelicals or Catholic—each group constituting about a quarter of the US population.[21]

While some may rejoice in this growing secularization of the American population, the implications for both social capital and personal happiness are dire. Religious *participation*, as opposed to *belief*, is an accurate predictor of numerous positive outcomes—including happiness and civic engagement. "People who are active in religious congregations tend to be happier and more civically engaged than either religiously unaffiliated adults or inactive members of religious groups," according to a major Pew Research Center study involving more than two dozen countries.[22]

Significantly, this relationship between religious participation and happiness holds across religions as well as across countries. Jews, Muslims, Christians, and those of other communal religious traditions are all more likely to report higher levels of happiness than their non-involved peers. And when it comes to social engagement, religiously active adults in the United States are nearly 20 percentage points more likely than the unaffiliated to participate in at least one other voluntary association.[23] The actively religious are also much more likely to vote, regardless of the country in which they live.

The downside of becoming a "none" is that such individuals are more likely to experience social isolation—and even alienation. In *Alienated America: Why Some Places Thrive While Others Collapse*, conservative writer Timothy Carney examines counties that were most likely to vote for Donald Trump in the 2016 Republican primary. Carney found that "Trump's support came disproportionally from those with low social connectedness."[24] More bluntly, "Trump did better in the primaries among people who didn't go to church."[25]

While Carney depicts the typical Trump primary voter as socially isolated and "unchurched," his harshest critique is reserved for the social dislocations that created the alienation. As well-paying factory jobs disappeared in America's heartland due to outsourcing and automation, alienation became "the disease of working-class America."[26] Once Mr. Trump identified those he believed to be responsible for what he termed "American carnage" (immigrants and China), he began to lock up the Republican nomination.

Carney, and other conservatives such as Yuval Levin and Arthur Brooks, are clear about what is required to restore the soul of America—a reinvigoration of the institutions of civil society. Carney notes that cohesive communities and a regular workplace are both institutions of civil society and that stable marriages are also key to healthy communities. Yuval Levin proposes that "we must revitalize the institutions that will enable vulnerable Americans to thrive."[27] And Arthur Brooks argues that "decent people can save America from the culture of contempt" if we learn to disagree well and elect "authoritative" rather than "coercive" leaders.[28]

In sum, civil society (and thus social capital) has been in dramatic decline since at least the 1990s. The decline in civil society, including participation in religious congregations, has accompanied and likely contributed to the rise in polarization. Thus, if we are to significantly reduce polarization, we will need to dramatically reverse the decline of civil society—including religion.

Summary

How do we go about transforming our current polarized paralysis into something more functional, more civil, and more hopeful? I believe that a four-step process—beginning with intrapersonal commitments and moving to interpersonal engagement and then to our congregations and communities—offers the greatest leverage for change. Intrapersonal changes inevitably impact our interpersonal relationships, and interpersonal relationships are what constitute our common life.

If we truly desire to transform our polarized relationships, congregations, and communities, we will need to learn from the Nassar family that holds to their land near Bethlehem while reaching out to their neighbors.

We will refuse to be enemies—and we will invite our neighbors to work together with us.

Notes

1. Friends of Tent of Nations North America, "People Building Bridges . . . Bridges of Peace!" (brochure), July 2018.

2. Taken from a description of Tent of Nations on the printed program when Daoud Nassar spoke at Eastern Mennonite Seminary (EMS), Harrisonburg, VA, November 8, 2018. All quotes from Daoud Nassar are also from his talk at EMS on November 8, 2018.
3. Timothy Seidel, "'We Refuse to Be Enemies': Political Geographies of Violence and Resistance in Palestine," *Journal of Peacebuilding and Development* 12, no. 3 (2017): 32.
4. Arthur C. Brooks, *Love Your Enemies: How Decent People Can Save America from the Culture of Contempt* (New York: Broadside Books, 2019), 41.
5. Donna Hicks, *Leading with Dignity: How to Create a Culture That Brings Out the Best in People* (New Haven: Yale University Press, 2018), 2.
6. Brooks, *Love Your Enemies*, 23.
7. Nationally, about two-thirds of Americans report that they support same-sex marriage as a legal right, but support is lower in many states in the southeastern United States. Wikipedia, s.v. "Public Opinion of Same Sex Marriage in the United States," accessed February 22, 2019, https://tinyurl.com/og8p5sn.
8. David R. Brubaker, "Recovering from Trauma in Congregations," *Perspectives*, Congregational Consulting Group, June 4, 2018, https://tinyurl.com/y46ygcy9.
9. Thomas Mann and Norman Ornstein, *It's Even Worse Than It Was: How the American Constitutional System Collided with the New Politics of Extremism* (Philadelphia: Basic Books, 2012).
10. Erik Maskin, "Five Reasons Ranked-Choice Voting Will Improve American Democracy," *Perspective Magazine*, December 4, 2018, https://tinyurl.com/y3akermh.
11. Katherine M. Gehl and Michael E. Porter, "Why Competition in the Politics Industry Is Failing America: A Strategy for Reinventing Our Democracy," Harvard Business School, September 2017, https://tinyurl.com/yc3bfzk4.
12. James Calvin Davis, *Forbearance: A Theological Ethic for a Disagreeable Church* (Grand Rapids: Eerdmans, 2017), 87.
13. Davis, *Forbearance*, 90.
14. David Gushee and Colin Holtz, *Moral Leadership for a Divided Age: 14 People Who Dared to Change Our World* (Grand Rapids: Brazos, 2018).
15. Jeff Brumley, "Sunday Morning Becoming the Most Politically 'Segregated' Hour in America," *Baptist News Global*, August 24, 2018, https://tinyurl.com/y4g5xx7h.
16. Yuval Levin, *The Fractured Republic: Renewing America's Social Contract in the Age of Individualism* (New York: Basic Books, 2016).
17. Levin, *The Fractured Republic*, 5.
18. Robert D. Putnam, *Bowling Alone: The Collapse and Revival of American Community* (New York: Simon & Schuster, 2000), 47.
19. Putnam, *Bowling Alone*, 66.

20. Robert D. Putnam and David E. Campbell, *American Grace: How Religion Divides and Unites Us* (New York: Simon & Schuster, 2010), 4.
21. Jack Jenkins, "'Nones' Now as Big as Catholics, Evangelicals in the US," *Religion News Service,* March 28, 2019, https://tinyurl.com/yygmvmyk.
22. Pew Research Center, "Religion's Relationship to Happiness, Civic Engagement, and Health around the World," January 31, 2019, https://tinyurl.com/yxv8r3yb.
23. Pew Research Center, "Religion's Relationship to Happiness."
24. Michael Barone, quoted in *Alienated America: Why Some Places Thrive While Others Collapse,* by Timothy P. Carney (New York: Harper Collins, 2019), 106.
25. Carney, *Alienated America,* 10.
26. Carney, *Alienated America,* 13.
27. Yuval Levin, *The Fractured Republic,* 126.
28. Brooks, *Love Your Enemies,* chapter 3.

7

LOVE THAT TRANSFORMS

David R. Brubaker

> We can only win the opponent over by love, never by hate.
> Hate is the subtlest form of violence.
> Hatred injures the hater, never the hated.
>
> —Mahatma Gandhi

Like other rabbis of his day, the teacher from Galilee attracted disciples (students) who decided to follow him in hopes of learning from and perhaps becoming like him. These followers represented the enormous range of the teacher's polarized society. One disciple, Matthew, was a former tax collector and a collaborator with the hated Roman occupiers. Another disciple, Simon the Zealot, likely identified with the freedom fighters who employed violence to resist Roman rule.[1]

The diversity among Jesus's disciples, which certainly included more than the twelve men named in the Christian Scriptures, would have been startling to Jesus's contemporaries. In addition to the varying backgrounds of the male disciples, women also numbered among Jesus's disciples. Several women—including Mary Magdalene, Joanna, and Susanna—are identified in the Gospel of Luke as followers and financial supporters of Jesus and his ministry.[2]

So this rabbi surprised people. Teaching and healing were standard practices for rabbis of Jesus's day. But including women, a tax collector, and a zealot among one's devoted disciples? And commanding followers to love even their enemies?

Jesus's "love for enemies" teaching came with a twist. Love for enemies included a commitment to challenge their dehumanizing behavior and the oppressive systems that supported such behavior. "If anyone forces you to go one mile, go also the second mile," Jesus instructed his followers.[3] Those listening would have understood this to be a clear reference to the prerogative of every Roman soldier to impress a civilian to carry his heavy pack for up to one mile. Theologian Walter Wink argues that a Roman military rule limited such impressment to a single mile, and if a civilian insisted on going "the second mile," the unpacked Roman soldier would fear consequences for violating the rule. According to Wink,

> [Jesus] is helping an oppressed people find a way to protest and neutralize an onerous practice despised throughout the empire. He is not giving a nonpolitical message of spiritual world transcendence. He is formulating a worldly spirituality in which the people at the bottom of society or under the thumb of imperial power learn to recover their humanity.[4]

This practice captures the paradox at the heart of successful depolarization efforts: loving challenge. It is not sufficient to love our enemies and passively accept their dehumanizing words and actions, as doing so ensures that nothing will change. At the same time, angry denunciations of the perpetrators and their unacceptable behaviors only cement our polarized divisions. When we are able to name and resist the systems that violate human dignity while affirming the dignity of those trapped in such systems, we are helping "to protest and neutralize" the onerous practices of our day. And when we form loving communities that reflect the broad diversity of our society, we are demonstrating that relationships can flourish even in age of polarization.

In this book, we endeavored to uncover the multiple causes of polarization and to identify responses that both enable resilience in the face of polarization and contribute to the transformation of our polarized reality. There are no quick fixes for a phenomenon that has been present in the United States since the country's founding and that has been metastasizing for the past forty years. However, there are increasing glimpses of successful leadership in the midst of our polarized age. Let's review what we've learned.

Understanding Polarization

Polarization happens when the center collapses as more and more people begin to occupy the poles at the ends of the normal curve. Although perspectives on any single issue can polarize a group of human beings, we tend to describe a social system as polarized when we observe that on any given issue, people take sides based on preexisting affiliations rather than on a process of discernment. When I choose my positions based primarily on whether a platform is labeled "Republican" or "Democratic," rather than on my own deepest values, I am participating in a process of partisan *political* polarization.

In chapter 1, we examined ten possible "drivers" of polarization found in the literature. What causes a family, congregation, or society to polarize? A summary follows.

Economic Inequality

The single greatest culprit driving political polarization may be growing economic stratification. Economic inequality strongly correlates with political polarization. As the gap between the richest and the poorest citizens increases, political polarization rises as well. Those countries with the greatest gap between the rich and the poor (such as Brazil) tend to experience the highest levels of political polarization, whereas the countries with the smallest wealth gaps (such as in northern Europe) experience lower levels of polarization.

Identity Threats

In social identity theory, the groups with which we identify are an important source not only of belonging but also of self-esteem. Thus, if individual members of an identity group feel their status is threatened, they are particularly likely to exhibit hostility toward other groups. Social identity theory and its concept of status threat help us understand why voters might respond to a leader who promises to reverse the real or perceived declining status of an identity group.

Racism and Racial Inequality

Racism may also be a significant driver of polarization. The legacy of enslavement and the reality of ongoing systemic racism produce profound racial inequities. According to the *Washington Post*, "white families have nearly 10 times the net worth of black families . . . and the gap is growing." Despite this reality, a majority of white Americans believe that they are victims of discrimination. Research suggests that voters respond positively to grievance narratives when they perceive members of a disadvantaged minority to be unfairly "getting ahead."

Sexism and Gender Inequality

Like racism, sexism and gender discrimination continue to infect American society. While there is a well-documented gender gap among American voters, as men are much more likely to vote Republican than are women, gender alone does not seem to be the prime contributor to polarization. The class gap between white college-educated women and white non–college educated women in 2016 was much larger than the gender gap between women and men.

Differing Moral Universes

Ethics professor Jonathan Haidt suggests that "morality is the key to understanding humanity."[5] Because every human being exists simultaneously as an individual and as part of a larger society, we are subject to "parochial altruism." Parochial altruism tends to produce generous and empathetic behaviors within a group but exclusionary or even violent behaviors with outsiders. The result can be a toxic tribalism or nationalism—a "my group, right or wrong" attitude that excludes or harms others. It's quite possible that those on the ends of our current polarized divide occupy two differing moral universes.

Global Nationalism and Wall-Building

Identity threat seems to be driving the rise in populism and nationalism around the world. One primary response to that threat is the growing worldwide pressure to limit immigration and to build walls. British author Tim Marshall charts the primary reason for building walls: fear. Whether designed to keep out the barbarians (ancient China) or the immigrants (United States and India), or to separate ethno-religious groups (Northern Ireland and Iraq), walls are generally built to reduce our anxieties. As genuine barriers, they often prove ineffective. As symbols of protection and exclusion, however, walls are remarkably powerful.

Balkanized Media

Numerous authors have identified the increasingly stratified media (Fox News vs. MSNBC) and polarized social media (such as affinity groups on Facebook) as the cause of polarization. Yet there is substantial evidence that the proliferation of news sources *reflects* increasing polarization even more than it *contributes* to it. First, social scientists have been tracking increasing polarization among the public since the early 1980s—well before Facebook, Twitter, and even Fox News were part of our daily lives. Second, the tendency of human beings to seek out evidence supporting our preexisting biases has been observed for millennia.

Political Structure

Perhaps the cause of modern polarization is our centuries-old "winner take all" political structure. Rather than establishing a parliamentary system that apportions representation based on the percentage of the vote obtained, the founders of the American republic designed a constitution that awards seats in Congress based purely on majority vote. An additional structural hypothesis is that partisan gerrymandering is the cause of the extreme polarization that we now see in Congress. However, while gerrymandering likely contributes to polarization, there is little evidence that it is a primary cause.

Social Sorting

Reporter Bill Bishop demonstrates that after 1976, Republicans and Democrats grew more geographically segregated. Unlike many authors on polarization, Bishop blames neither politicians nor the media for our current divides. The problem is that growing homogeneity corresponds with increasing extremism, as individuals who participate in only like-minded groups or live in like-minded neighborhoods tend to develop more partisan views. Bishop blames not gerrymandering but gentrification and other social trends for the increase in congressional districts primarily composed of like-minded people.

Leadership-Driven Polarization

The final possible cause of our polarized era is a leader who foments polarization. Top political leaders occupy a paradoxical position. They are both contributors to and symbols of developments in their countries. Countries do not elect highly polarizing leaders unless they are in a highly polarized, or desperate, state. In the United States, many Trump voters felt threatened and marginalized, fearing that they were losing their place in the country and wanting to "make American great again." Thus, the most significant contribution of leaders may be to give *voice* to the already-felt grievances of members of the populace.

We thus concluded that one route to societal polarization lies through the combination of economic inequality, identity threat, and leaders who articulate the felt grievances of those who believe they are losing out. The formula, again, looks like this:

INCOME INEQUALITY + IDENTITY THREAT + ARTICULATED GRIEVANCE = POLARIZATION

Leadership and Polarization

We then considered the debilitating impact on those who are called to lead in a polarized environment. Based on two case studies (of a university president and a lead pastor/community leader) as well as insights from top leadership authors, we identified four "C's" for surviving and even thriving in an age of polarization.

Clarity

Leaders who succeed in an age of polarization demonstrate clarity at two levels—within themselves and with others. Internal clarity requires that leaders know and act on their core values and principles. Clarity within begets clarity with others. When we know who we are and what we believe, we naturally communicate that clarity to others. This is not an attempt to convert others to one's beliefs. Rather, it is an expression of candor or *transparency*—a willingness to reveal our inner thoughts and beliefs to others.

Compassion

Compassion and clarity belong together. Clarity compels us to speak with conviction. Compassion invites us to listen with concentration. It is in the dance between clarity and compassion that leaders build trust. We tend to respect those leaders who know what they believe yet are equally interested in learning about our beliefs and experiences. Genuine compassion also requires that leaders understand the multiple sources of identity and life experiences that shape the radically different perspectives of human beings.

Courage

Polarized times demand courageous leadership—in universities, businesses, congregations, nonprofit organizations, and government. Dr. Loren Swartzendruber's story illustrates the courage required to initiate a listening-and-change process on a highly polarized issue within a university. Courageous leadership requires entering the storm of conflict while holding tight to one's convictions and compassion.

Connection

Leaders who survive and thrive in polarized environments exhibit clarity, compassion, courage, and connection. Such leaders begin with an internal connection to their own values, beliefs, and emotions. They are then able to connect with those they are leading and with the communities in which they live and work. Finally, they strive to stay connected even with their enemies. Staying connected with our enemies requires an acknowledgment that they too possess basic dignity.

The story of Faith in Action, and Rev. Davis Sensenig's leadership of this interfaith organization, demonstrates that connection may have the greatest impact at the community level. While structured dialogue processes have their place, it is in the process of *working* together (even more than *talking* together) that genuine bonds of friendship are forged.

Communicating across the Divide

In chapter 3, Everett Brubaker addressed the power of language to both divide and connect, and described the tendency of the English language to narrate our reality in binary terms. He then urged that we adopt a "mindfulness of language" to overcome this linguistic limitation. If we know our language favors polarity and has led to entirely different ways of speaking about an issue, Brubaker concludes, it is critical that we be intentional about the words we use and mindful of their potential impact.

Brubaker examined three classic pillars of communication theory—the message, the messenger, and the audience—and the importance of accounting for the moral foundations and values systems of those listening. Messages designed to appeal only to the "true believers" while shaming and alienating those of a different persuasion only contribute to increasing polarization. If we wish to successfully reach across the divide, we will need to practice dialogue that seeks to understand another and build relationship.

Trauma and Resilience: The Missing Factors

The relationship between polarization and trauma is starting to be explored, and in chapters 4 and 5 Carolyn Yoder and Teresa Haase offered significant contributions to our understanding. To understand trauma, Yoder suggested, we need to begin with our physical body, specifically the nervous system/brain. Unaddressed trauma may lie at the root of many of our polarized social systems—whether families, congregations or other organizations, communities, or entire societies.

This understanding will lead us in new directions in our quest to depolarize American society. It will be necessary to address the systemic enslavement of Africans violently transported to the Americas and brutally mistreated here, as well as the systemic genocide against Native Americans. We must also acknowledge that the legacy of our Civil War continues to inflame regional conflicts and to spawn Southern resentment. And we will need to respond to the millions of veterans who returned from wars in Europe, Asia, and the Middle East since 1941 and who continue to suffer from heightened levels of both PTSD and suicide.[6]

Our families, congregations, and communities may also need assistance in naming and recovering from past or ongoing traumas that spawn polarization. Yoder suggests that if you want to know if unaddressed trauma is affecting you, your community, or organization, observe the *quality of the relationships* people have with themselves and each other over months, years, and centuries. If those relationships reflect aspects of the cycles of violence diagram depicted in chapter 4, unresolved trauma may be at the root of the polarized relationships.

While an awareness of trauma is core to understanding why some relationships polarize, the practice of *resilience* enables leaders and others to endure. Haase suggested that resilience is the process of bouncing back from hardship or failure. She reviewed the core practices of resiliency—including stress-tolerance, self-awareness, vulnerability, embrace of the unknown, and ingenuity.

In order to weather the storm of leading in an age of polarization, leaders must practice self-care and find ways to make meaning in the midst of the surrounding turbulence. As Haase observed, making meaning is what makes us human, and polarization at its worst creates an environment where it is easy to dehumanize each other and where fear is the driving force. In our current polarized environment there is no substitute for the practice of resilience.

Transforming Polarization

In chapter 6, we suggested specific steps that individuals can take to overcome polarizing tendencies in ourselves, our relationships, and our social systems.

Within ourselves, we can start by refusing to hold others in contempt, by honoring the inherent dignity of every human being, and by broadening our thinking and speaking beyond the binaries of our typical discourse. In the context of our relationships, we can commit to seeking first to understand (before trying to be understood), inviting disagreement, and staying connected in the midst of disagreements.

As leaders in our congregations and other organizations, we can work to unearth the underlying issues (rather than overfocusing on the identified issue), strengthen the connections among leaders, and examine the historical patterns (including historical traumas) that may be keeping us stuck. Within our communities and society, we can work with others to change the political culture and structure, transform the religious and social culture, and, perhaps most importantly, rebuild civil society.

Religious congregations gather the most people, and thus are the most significant, of all sectors of civil society in the United States today. Therefore, there is no more important venue where we can work to rebuild civil society than in and among religious congregations. Ecumenical cooperation and interfaith collaborations, such as the organization Faith in Action described in chapter 2, thus emerge as the primary mechanisms for rebuilding civil society in any community. As we restore civil society community by community, our society will also begin to heal.

Conclusion

Do you want to be part of depolarizing your family, organization, community, or society? Here are five of the most effective ways to do so. Choose one and begin implementing it, with others, today.

1. *Within yourself*, refuse contempt, honor dignity, and broaden binaries. *With others*, seek first to understand, invite disagreement, and stay connected. I'm part of a "Gang of Six" at my local Mennonite congregation that meets once a month to talk about our similarities and our differences. The group formed in 2016 when a conserva-

tive friend and I agreed to gather four others with differing theological and political perspectives to talk about our beliefs and what led us to embrace them. The result is a group that I look forward to connecting with each month and that has broadened my understanding of and respect for what more traditional Christians think and believe.

2. Connect with a local religious congregation or other civic organization or strengthen your existing connection to your current congregation or association. Then encourage your congregation to be part of ecumenical and interfaith initiatives in your community, or lead your association in connecting with other groups in your community. It is possible to reweave our connections at the local level, as Faith in Action is doing in Harrisonburg, Virginia. But doing so requires a commitment to ecumenical and interfaith relationships, and an understanding that genuine change involves a long game.
3. Collaborate with others to identify and surface underlying trauma or dysfunction that may be keeping your congregation or other organization stuck in unhealthy patterns. This process will require both the support of organizational leaders and the expertise of outside professionals with training in trauma awareness and resilience. Trauma is the glue that keeps many congregations and other organizations stuck in polarizing patterns. Unsticking that glue will require both naming the underlying trauma and agreeing on new patterns of relating that will lead to greater health.
4. Deliberately initiate or work to strengthen relationships with other individuals and groups that you know do not share your own beliefs and assumptions about the world. Since one-off conversations seldom lead to any change, agree on an ongoing process of engagement and dialogue. This normally requires both clear ground rules and constructive facilitation, but not necessarily outside professionals. One organization that supports such efforts is Better Angels, which seeks to "form new relationships across the divide."[7]
5. Support and advocate for local and national initiatives that seek greater economic equality and enhanced safety and security for all. Since economic inequality and identity threat are two of the main drivers of polarization, public policy initiatives to enhance economic security and to reduce fear will ultimately be required to fully overcome our current polarization. The United States faces a fundamental choice: Will it become a "dual economy" character-

> ized by a wealthy elite and an impoverished majority, or will it become a society where "the gap between the haves and the have-nots has been narrowed?"[8] These are essentially public policy choices.

Can we overcome the polarization we are now enduring? Yes, but it will require genuine change at all of the levels described in the Dugan nested model in the introduction—relationships, subsystems (congregations, organizations, and communities), and systems (our societies and world). As much as we would like to lay all of the blame for our current fractured society at the feet of politicians and the media, doing so also frees us of any responsibility for fixing our broken systems.

If we wish to contribute to depolarizing our society, we need to be part of diverse, loving communities that confront oppressive structures while refusing to demonize the individuals who occupy them. This is the model that Jesus revealed in Palestine, Mahatma Gandhi incorporated in India, and Martin Luther King Jr. embodied in the United States. The model is not dependent on a charismatic leader. It does, however, depend on one essential insight: that we can only change what we first love.

Notes

1. Very little is known about Simon the Zealot, and some scholars suggest Simon may have obtained the descriptor "zealot" due to his "zeal" for his religion rather than for his opposition to Roman rule. See Wikipedia, s.v. Simon the Zealot, https://tinyurl.com/y4d4enc3.
2. Luke 8:1–3.
3. Matthew 5:41.
4. Walter Wink, *The Powers That Be: Theology for a New Millennium* (New York: Doubleday, 1998), 101.
5. Jonathan Haidt, *The Righteous Mind: Why Good People Are Divided by Politics and Religion* (New York: Vintage Books, 2013), 231.
6. U.S. Department of Veterans Affairs, "Veteran Suicide Data," 2016, https://tinyurl.com/y6fk4wws.
7. Better Angels, www.better-angels.org.
8. Joseph E. Stiglitz, *The Price of Inequality: How Today's Divided Society Endangers Our Future* (New York: W. W. Norton, 2013), 362.

BIBLIOGRAPHY

Abadi, Mark. "Democrats and Republicans Speak Different Languages—and It Helps Explain Why We're So Divided." *Business Insider*, August 11, 2017, https://tinyurl.com/y32onrao.

Abramowitz, Alan I. *The Disappearing Center*. New Haven: Yale University Press, 2010.

———. *The Polarized Public? Why American Government Is So Dysfunctional*. Upper Saddle River, NJ: Pearson, 2013.

Advisory Committee on Colleague Assistance. "Shared Trauma: Helping Clients Cope with National Events That Affect the Therapist." *American Psychological Association*, 2019, https://tinyurl.com/y38vjvky.

Allen, Melanie. "Dealing with Ambiguity and Developing Resilience." Melanie Allen Life Coaching and Career Development, 2019, https://tinyurl.com/y5osvr7n.

American Psychiatric Association. *Diagnostic and Statistical Manual of Mental Disorders, Vol 5*. New York: American Psychiatric Publishing, 2013.

Anderson, Carol. *White Rage: The Unspoken Truth of Our Racial Divide*. New York: Bloomsbury, 2017.

Anderson, Mary B., and Marshall Wallace. *Opting Out of War: Strategies to Prevent Violent Conflict*. Boulder, CO: Lynne Rienner, 2013.

Atlee, Tom. "Polarization, Conversation, and Collective Intelligence." *Integral Leadership Review*, 2018, https://tinyurl.com/o3j3w4y.

Ballotpedia. "Winner-Take-All," 2018, https://tinyurl.com/yxduv52x.

Birner, Betty. "Does the Language I Speak Influence the Way I Think?" *Linguistic Society of America*, 2019, https://tinyurl.com/y5cnv63y.

Bishop, Bill. *The Big Sort: Why the Clustering of Like-Minded People Is Tearing Us Apart*. New York: Mariner, 2008.

Blankenhorn, David. "The Top 14 Causes of Political Polarization." *The American Interest*, May 16, 2018, https://tinyurl.com/y883t4w7.

Booker, Betty. "Blind Trust Author: Leaders' Actions in Crisis Impel Conflict, Peace." *Richmond Dispatch*, October 4, 2004.

Boroditsky, Lera, Caitlin Fausey, and Bria Long. "The Role of Language in Eye-Witness Memory: Remembering Who Did It in English and Japanese." *Proceedings of the Annual Meeting of the Cognitive Science Society*, 2426–31. Merced, California: UC Merced, 2009.

Botcharova, Olga. "Implementation of Track Two Diplomacy." In *Forgiveness and Reconciliation*. Edited by Raymond G. Helmick and Rodney L. Petersen. Radnor, PA: Templeton Foundation Press, 2001.

Bradlee, Ben. *The Forgotten: How the People of One Pennsylvania County Elected Donald Trump and Changed America*. New York: Little Brown, 2018.

Bragt, Thieleman Van. *Martyrs Mirror: The Story of Seventeen Centuries of Christian Martyrdom from the Time of Christ to A.D. 1660*. Scottdale, PA: Herald, 2010.

Brooks, Arthur C. *Love Your Enemies: How Decent People Can Save America from the Culture of Contempt*. New York: Broadside, 2019.

———. "Sick and Tired of the Culture of Contempt: Here Are Five Ways You Can Subvert It." *Ideas.Ted.com*, April 10, 2019, http://tinyurl.com/y44jcl76.

Brown, Brené. *Dare to Lead: Daring Greatly and Rising Strong at Work*. New York: Random House, 2018.

———. *Daring Greatly: How the Courage to Be Vulnerable Transforms the Way We Live, Love, Parent, and Lead*. London: Penguin, 2016.

———. "Strong Back, Soft Front, Wild Heart." *On Being with Krista Tippett*, February 8, 2018, https://tinyurl.com/ycn7qmwt.

Brownley, Travis. "The Necessity of Stress." *Heads and Tales at Marin Academy*, December 12, 2013, https://tinyurl.com/pzpxllo.

Brubaker, David R. "Recovering from Trauma in Congregations." *Congregational Consulting Group*, June 4, 2018, https://tinyurl.com/y46ygcy9.

Brubaker, Everett N. "No, We're Not Kidding: Environmental Messaging by Conservatives, for Conservatives." *Western States Communication Association Annual Conference*. Seattle: Unpublished Paper, 2019.

Brumley, Jeff. "Sunday Morning Becoming the Most Politically 'Segregated' Hour in America." *Baptist News Global*, August 24, 2018, https://tinyurl.com/y4g5xx7h.

Buber, Martin. *I and Thou*. New York: Scribner, 1958.

Business Insider. "This 60-Second Animation Shows How Divided Congress Has Become Over the Last 60 Years." YouTube video, 1:24. Uploaded May 11, 2016, http://tinyurl.com/y4uyvacy.

Carney, Timothy P. *Alienated America: Why Some Places Thrive While Others Collapse*. New York: HarperCollins, 2019.

Cassino, Dan. "Emasculation, Conservatism, and the 2016 Election." *Context* 17, no. 1 (2018): 48–53.

CDC-Kaiser Permanente. "About the CDC-Kaiser ACE Study." *Centers for Disease Control and Prevention*, June 14, 2016, http://tinyurl.com/y4bzvslx.

Center for Ethical Leadership. "Self-Guided Core Values Assessment," 2002, https://tinyurl.com/zz5p3q6.

Chen, Agnes. "How Learning to Be Vulnerable Can Make Life Safer." *Invisibilia*. National Public Radio, June 17, 2016, https://tinyurl.com/y773wfkf.

Chua, Amy. *Political Tribes: Group Instinct and the Fate of Nations*. New York: Penguin, 2018.

Coutu, Diane. "How Resilience Works." *Harvard Business Review*, 2002, https://tinyurl.com/pcpsk8o.

Cox, David. "The Edwin Friedman Model of Family Systems Thinking." *Academic Leadership: The Online Journal* 4, no. 4 (Fall 2006).

Crawford, Krysten. "American Political Speech Is Increasingly Partisan, Stanford Research Shows." *Stanford News*, July 19, 2016, https://tinyurl.com/y4a3wyal.

Creamer, Robert. "To Reduce Political Polarization in Washington, We Must Reduce the Economic Polarization of America." *Facts and Arts*, January 11, 2010, https://tinyurl.com/y344najz.

Dana, Deb. "Beginners Guide to Polyvagal Theory." *debdanalcsw.com*, 2018, http://tinyurl.com/y5bc8tlj.

———. *The Polyvagal Theory in Therapy: Engaging the Rhythm of Regulation*. New York: W. W. Norton, 2018.

Davis, James Calvin. *Forbearance: A Theological Ethic for a Disagreeable Church*. Grand Rapids: Eerdmans, 2017.

Desilver, Drew. "For Most U.S. Workers, Real Wages Have Barely Budged in Decades." *Pew Research Center*, August 7, 2018, https://tinyurl.com/ycxhufef.

Dews, Fred. "A Primer on Gerrymandering and Political Polarization." *Brookings Now*, July 6, 2017, https://tinyurl.com/yd62vtc2.

DiAngelo, Robin. *White Fragility: Why It's So Hard for White People to Talk about Racism*. Boston: Beacon, 2018.

Donnelly, Grace. "Top CEOs Make More in Two Days Than an Average Employee Does in One Year." *Fortune*, July 20, 2017, https://tinyurl.com/y85vz6gn.

Dugan, Maire A. "A Nested Theory of Conflict." *A Leadership Journal* 1 (July 1996).

Eastern Mennonite University, "EMU's Diversity Timeline," 2018, https://tinyurl.com/y4zz2njt.

Ely, Robin J., and Debra Meyerson. "Unmasking Manly Men." *Harvard Business Review*, 2008, https://tinyurl.com/yy6z7ml6.

Entman, Robert M. "Framing toward Clarification of a Fractured Paradigm." *Journal of Communication* 43, no. 4 (1991): 51–58.

Escobar, Oliver. *Public Dialogue and Deliberation*. Edinburgh: Edinburgh Beltane, 2011.

Essential Partners. "Conversations across the Red-Blue Divide," 2018, https://tinyurl.com/yyeqxqpl.

Estes, Clarissa Pinkola. "Letter to a Young Activist during Troubled Times." *Maven Productions*, 2018, https://tinyurl.com/y64w7ayl.

Flick, Deborah L. *From Debate to Dialogue: Using the Understanding Process to Transform our Conversations*. Boulder, CO: Orchid Publications, 1998.

Frankl, Viktor. *Man's Search for Meaning*. Boston: Beacon, 2006.

Friedersdorf, Conor. "A Better Way to Look at Most Every Political Issue." *The Atlantic*, February 11, 2018, https://tinyurl.com/y7lkqt79.

Friedman, Thomas L. "Where American Politics Can Still Work: From the Ground Up." *New York Times*, July 3, 2018, https://tinyurl.com/y72td8m2.

Gajewski, Misha. "May I Take Your Metaphor? How We Talk about Cancer." *Cancer Research UK*, September 28, 2015, https://tinyurl.com/yxkpsscw.

Gamble, Teri K., and Michael Gamble. *Communication Works*. New York: McGraw-Hill, 2013.

Gehl, Katherine M., and Michael E. Porter. *Why Competition in the Politics Industry Is Failing America: A Strategy for Reinventing our Democracy*. Cambridge, MA: Harvard Business School, 2017.

Geier, Kathleen. "Inquality among Women Is Crucial to Understanding Hillary's Loss." *The Nation*, November 11, 2016, https://tinyurl.com/j3l6gag.

Gentzkow, Matthew, Jesse M. Shapiro, and Matt Taddy. "Measuring Group Difference in High-Dimensional Choices: Method and Application to Congressional Speech." National Bureau of Economic Research, March 2019, http://tinyurl.com/y6m8mcw3.

Giacoman, Augusto. "The Strength of Vulnerable Leaders." *Strategy + Business*, November 29, 2017, https://tinyurl.com/yyyrrkhk.

Gilmore, Susan, and Patrick Fraleigh. *The Friendly Style Profile for People at Work*. Booklet. Eugene, OR: Friendly Press, 2004. https://tinyurl.com/yc22cd5t.

Glaude, Eddie S. "Our Racist Soul." *Time*, September 17, 2018, 42–45.

Gonyea, Don. "Majority of White Americans Say They Believe Whites Face Discrimination." National Public Radio, October 24, 2017, https://tinyurl.com/y9n7jbw2.

Goodwin, Doris Kearns. *Leadership in Turbulent Times*. New York: Simon & Schuster, 2018.

Graf, Nikki, Anna Brown, and Eileen Patten. "The Narrowing, but Persisent, Gender Gap in Pay." *Pew Research Center*, April 9, 2018, https://tinyurl.com/y49w5sjg.

Graham, Jesse, Jonathan Haidt, and Brian A. Nosek. "Liberals and Conservatives Rely on Different Sets of Moral Foundations." *Journal of Personality and Social Psychology* 96, no. 5 (2009): 1029–46.

Greenberg, Melanie. "Americans Just Broke a New Record for Stress and Anxiety." *Psychology Today*, February 19, 2017, https://tinyurl.com/y35f32f6.

Gushee, David, and Colin Holtz. *Moral Leadership for a Divided Age: 14 People Who Dared to Change Our World*. Grand Rapids: Brazos, 2018.

Haidt, Jonathan. *The Righteous Mind: Why Good People Are Divided by Politics and Religion*. New York: Vintage, 2012.

Hart, Drew G. *Trouble I've Seen: Changing the Way the Church Views Racism*. Scottdale, PA: Herald, 2016.

Hayakawa, S. I. *Language in Thought and Action*. Oxford: Harcourt, Brace, 1949.

Hicks, Donna. *Leading with Dignity: How to Create a Culture That Brings Out the Best in People*. New Haven: Yale University Press, 2018.

Hill, Napoleon. "Our Strongest Oaks." *The Strongest Oak*, 2017, https://tinyurl.com/y3mhvhtq.

Hooker, David Anderson, and Amy Potter Czajkowski. "Transforming Historical Harms." *Coming to the Table*, October 1, 2013, http://tinyurl.com/y2rt5cyd.

Jakobson, Roman. *Linguistics and Poetics in Style in Language*. Cambridge, MA: MIT Press, 1960.

Jan, Tracey. "White Families Have Nearly 10 Times the Wealth of Black Families. And the Gap Is Growing." *Washington Post*, September 28, 2017, https://tinyurl.com/y4ct72wr.

Jenkins, Jack. "'Nones' Now as Big as Catholics, Evangelicals in the U.S." *Religion News Service*, March 21, 2019, https://tinyurl.com/yygmvmyk.

Jenkins, Nash. "Why Did the Philippines Just Elect a Guy Who Jokes about Rape as Its President?" *Time*, May 10, 2016, https://tinyurl.com/j4yc3ac.

Johnson, Barry. *Polarity Management: Identifying and Solving Unsolvable Problems*. Amherst, MA: HRD Press, 2014.

Junger, Sebastian. *Tribe: On Homecoming and Belonging*. New York: Hachette, 2016.

Kellow, Christine L., and H. Leslie Steeves. "The Role of Radio in the Rwandan Genocide." *Journal of Communication* 48, no. 3 (September 1998): 107–28.

Khazan, Olga. "Inherited Trauma Shapes Your Health." *The Atlantic*, October 16, 2018, http://tinyurl.com/y6r7tbqf.

———. "People Voted for Trump Because They Were Anxious, Not Poor." *The Atlantic*, April 23 2018, https://tinyurl.com/y89uqrm9.

Leas, Speed. "Levels of Conflict." *The Center for Congregational Health*, September 1, 2011, http://tinyurl.com/y6applv3.

Levin, Yuval. *The Fractured Republic: Renewing America's Social Contract in the Age of Individualism*. New York: Basic, 2016.

Levinson, Stephen C. "Language and Cognition: The Cognitive Consequences of Spatial Description in Guugu Yimithirr." *Journal of Linguistic Anthropology* 7, no. 1 (1997): 98–131.

Lisitsa, Ellie. "The Four Horsemen: Criticism, Contempt, Defensiveness, and Stonewalling." *The Gottman Institute*, April 23, 2013, https://tinyurl.com/jfnk7xf.

Mack, John E. "The Enemy System." In *The Psychodynamics of International Relationships*, vol. 1, *Concepts and Theories*. Edited by Vamik D. Volkan, Demetrios A. Julius and Joseph V. Montville. Lexington, VA: Lexington Books, 1990.

———. Foreword in *Cyprus: War and Adaptation: A Psychoanalytic History of*

Two Ethnic Groups in Conflict, by Vamik Volkan. Charlottesville: University of Virginia Press, 1979.

Makau, Josina M., and Debian L. Marty. *Dialogue and Deliberation*. Long Grove, IL: Waveland, 2013.

Mann, Thomas, and Norman Ornsein. *It's Even Worse Than It Was: How the American Constitutional System Collided with the New Politics of Extremism*. Philadelphia: Basic, 2012.

Marshall, Tim. *Divided: Why We're Living in an Age of Walls*. London: Elliott & Thompson, 2018.

Maskin, Erik. "Five Reasons Ranked-Choice Voting Will Improve American Democracy." *Perspective Magazine, The Boston Globe*, December 4, 2018, https://tinyurl.com/y3akermh.

Mason, Lillianna. *Uncivil Agreement: How Politics Became Our Identity*. Chicago: University of Chicago Press, 2018.

Maxwell, John. "Leading in Polarized Times." *JohnMaxwell.com*, November 13, 2018, https://tinyurl.com/y3vn9fxx.

McCarty, Nolan, Keith T Poole, and Howard Rosenthal. *Polarized America: The Dance of Ideology and Unequal Riches*. Cambridge, MA: MIT Press, 2016.

McCright, Aaron M., and Riley E. Dunlap. "The Politicization of Climate Change and Polarization in the American Public's View of Global Warming, 2001–2010." *The Sociological Quarterly* 52, no. 2 (2011): 155–94.

McPherson, Miller, Lynn Smith Lovin, and James M. Cook. "Birds of a Feather: Homophily in Social Networks." *Annual Review of Sociology* 27 (August 2001): 415–44.

Meacham, Jon. *The Soul of America: The Battle for Our Better Angels*. New York: Random House, 2018.

Menakem, Resmaa. *My Grandmother's Hands: Racialized Trauma and the Pathway to Mending Our Hearts and Bodies*. Las Vegas: Central Recovery Press, 2017.

Metz, Steven. "The Rise of Identity Populism Is Making the World More Dangerous." *World Politics Review*, November 2, 2018, http://tinyurl.com/y3svg3rt.

Monmouth University. "Climate Concerns Increase; Most Republicans Now Acknowledge Change." *Monmouth University Polling Institute*, November 29, 2018, https://tinyurl.com/y2s3m7e5.

Mozur, Paul. "A Genocide Incited on Facebook, with Posts from Myanmar's Military." *New York Times*, October 15, 2018, http://tinyurl.com/y346l2f6.

Mulhall, Robert. "Leading with Vulnerability: How Being Vulnerable Can Serve—not Harm—You as a Leader." *The Crossland Group*, 2019, https://tinyurl.com/y6j56p7d.

National Issues Forums. "A House Divided: What Would We Have to Give Up to Get the Political System We Want." *National Issues Forums*, 2019, https://tinyurl.com/y48qy87r.

Oudshoorn, Judah, Michelle Jackett, and Lorraine Stutzman. *The Little Book of Restorative Justice for Sexual Abuse: Hope through Trauma*. New York: Good Books, 2015.

Paquette, Danielle. "The Unexpected Voters Behind the Largest Gender Gap in Recorded Election History." *Washington Post*, November 9, 2016, https://tinyurl.com/yyu7p8es.

Pascual, Shelley. "The Gruesome Story of a Radical ISIS-Like Movement That Once Ruled Münster." *The Local*, May 3, 2018, http://tinyurl.com/y5rocwnm.

Pew Research Center. "Religion's Relationship to Happiness, Civic Engagement, and Health around the World," January 31, 2019, https://tinyurl.com/yxv8r3yb.

Porges, Stephen W. *The Pocket Guide to the Polyvagal Theory: The Transofrmative Power of Feeling Safe*. New York: W. W. Newton, 2017.

PsychAlive, "What Is the Polyvagal Theory." YouTube video, 4:10. Uploaded April 23, 2018, https://tinyurl.com/yy6wnyms.

Putnam, Robert D. *Bowling Alone: The Collapse and Revival of American Community*. New York: Simon & Schuster, 2000.

Putnam, Robert D., and David E. Campbell. *American Grace: How Religion Divides and Unites Us*. New York: Simon & Schuster, 2010.

Rohr, Richard. *Everything Belongs*. New York: Crossroads, 2003.

Rosenfeld, Sam. *The Polarizers: Postwar Architects of Our Partisan Era*. Chicago: University of Chicago Press, 2018.

Sanders, Richard. "The Myth of 'Shock and Awe': Why the Iraqi Invasion Was a Disaster." *The Telegraph*, March 19, 2013, https://tinyurl.com/y5bdlc2h.

Sasse, Ben. *Them: Why We Hate Each Other—and How to Heal*. New York: St. Martin's, 2018.

Seidel, Timothy. "'We Refuse to Be Enemies': Political Geographies of Violence and Resistance in Palestine." *Journal of Peacebuilding and Development* 12, no. 3 (2017): 25–38.

Seltzer, Leon. "How Vulnerable Should You Let Yourself Be?" *Psychology Today*, January 3, 2018, https://tinyurl.com/y4y8xf8d.

Shaw, Colin. "Dealing with Ambiguity: The New Business Imperative." *Beyond Philosophy Blog*, September 9, 2013, https://tinyurl.com/y43jyk4u.

Shmueli, Deborah, Michael Elliott, and Sanda Kaufman. "Frame Changes and the Management of Intractable Conflicts." *Conflict Resolution Quarterly* 24, no. 2 (2006): 207–18.

Sides, John, and Lynn Vavreck Michael Tesler. *Identity Crisis: The 2016 Presidential Campaign and the Battle for the Meaning of America*. Princeton, NJ: Princeton University Press, 2018.

Siegel, Daniel J. *Pocket Guide to Interpersonal Neurobiology: An Integrative Handbook of the Mind* . New York: W. W. Norton, 2012.

Sinek, Simon. *Leaders Eat Last: Why Some Teams Pull Together and Others Don't*. New York: Penguin, 2017.

Stauffer, Holly. "Harrisonburg City Council Passes "Welcome America" Resolution by Faith in Action." *WHSV*, August 24, 2016, https://tinyurl.com/y3huv6py.

Stewart, James B. "Why Trump's Unusual Leadership Style Isn't Working in the White House." *New York Times*, January 10, 2019, https://tinyurl.com/y8emh4jd.

Stiglitz, Joseph E. *The Price of Inequality: How Today's Divided Society Endangers Our Future*. New York: W. W. Norton, 2013.

Stone, Chad, Danilo Trisi, Arloc Sherman, and Roderick Taylor. "A Guide to Statistics on Historical Trends in Income Inequality." *Center on Budget and Policy Priorities*. August 29, 2018.

Syverson, Tom. "Linguistics Can Help Conservatives and Liberals Agree on Objective Reality Again." *Quartz*, February 23, 2017, https://tinyurl.com/h7s32uw.

Tarver, Michael. "Why Did Venezuelans Elect Hugo Chavez President?" *History Hit Podcast with Michael Tarver*, September 18, 2018, https://tinyurl.com/y3ofyusc.

Tennant, Ella. "How Gendered Language Shapes the Way We See the World." *Phys.org*, November 29, 2017, https://tinyurl.com/y6pc56m5.

US Department of Veterans Affairs. "Mental Health," 2019, https://tinyurl.com/y6fk4wws.

Vivian, Pat, and Shana Hormann. *Organizational Trauma and Healing*. Scotts Valley, CA: CreateSpace, 2013.

Volkan, Vamik. *Blind Trust: Large Groups and Their Leaders in Times of Crisis and Terror*. Durham: Pitchstone, 2004.

———. "Transgenerational Transmissions and Chosen Traumas: An Aspect of Large Group Identity." *Group Analysis* 34, no. 1 (March 2001): 79–97.

Wink, Walter. *The Powers That Be*. New York: Harmony, 2010.

Winkler, Hernan. "The Effect of Income Inequality on Political Polarization: Evidence from European Regions, 2002–2014." *Economics and Politics* 31, no. 2 (July 2019): 1–26.

Wolsko, Christopher. "Expanding the Range of Environmental Values: Political Orientation, Moral Foundations, and the Common Ingroup." *Journal of Environmental Psychology* 51 (2017): 284–94.

Yale University. "Climate Change Opinions Rebound among Republican Voters." *Yale Program on Climate Change Communication*, May 8, 2018, https://tinyurl.com/yxfq6eyj.

Yoder, Carolyn. *The Little Book of Trauma Healing:: When Violence Strikes and Community Security Is Threatened*. New York: Good Books, 2005.

Zhou, Jack. "Boomerangs versus Javelins: How Polarization Constrains Communication on Climate Change." *Environmental Politics* 25, no. 5 (2016): 788–811.